D1799961

Carl-Auer

Entering Inner Images

Eva Madelung/Barbara Innecken

A Creative Use of Constellations in Individual Therapy,
Counselling, Groups and Self-Help

Translated by Colleen Beaumont

2004

Published by Carl-Auer-Systeme Verlag: **www.carl-auer.com**
Please order our catalogue:

Carl-Auer-Systeme Verlag
Weberstrasse 2
69120 Heidelberg
Germany

Cover: WSP Design, Heidelberg
Cover Image: M. C. Escher's "Swans"
© 2004 The M. C. Escher Company - Baarn - Holland. All rights reserved.
Printed by Koninklijke Wöhrmann B. V., Zutphen
Printed in The Netherlands

ISBN 3-89670-439-7

Copyright © 2004 by Carl-Auer-Systeme
All rights reserved. No part of this book may be reproduced by any process
whatsoever without the written permission of the copyright owner.

Title of the original edition:
„Im Bilde sein"
© 2003 by Carl-Auer-Systeme, Heidelberg

Bibliographic information published by Die Deutschen Bibliothek
Die Deutsche Bibliothek lists this publication
in the Deutsche Nationalbibliografie; detailed bibliographic
data is available in the Internet at http://dnb.ddb.de.

Contents

Foreword

When I first came to this book, I was already familiar with the systemic-constructivist model, work with constellations, and the solution orientation of Steve de Shazer's approach. I knew somewhat less about Neuro-Linguistic Programming (NLP). Neuro-Imaginative Gestalting (NIG) consists of an artful and harmonious blend of elements taken from these four approaches and creatively developed by Eva Madelung and, consequently, I was not expecting to find much that was new to me in this book by Eva Madelung and Barbara Innecken.

The book took me by surprise and I discovered otherwise. It confirmed again for me, that through a creative combining of known elements, it is possible to create something innovative and stimulating that is then receptive to further development.

This book is also proof that one can present complex procedures in a way that is clear and accessible to readers and practitioners. Particularly for those who rely on language as their primary medium in therapy and counselling, NIG offers a wide variety of visual methods and exercises. The reader finds himself eager to try them out immediately. Additionally, the attention to differentiated physical perceptions provides access to a more extensive experience of differences and relationships. This provides a broader, more diverse spectrum in one's approach to clients.

It is a treat that the introduction to the theoretical bases is held within limits, without starting back at Adam and Eve. The basic premises behind the applied method are presented briefly, in meaningful relation to each other and to the applications in NIG, and differences and common features noted. Due to the condensed presentation of the theoretical background, it sometimes assumes the compressed outlines of a woodcutting, and complexities are, of course, simplified; however the more comprehensive literature is signposted.

Eva Madelung and Barbara Innecken rightfully concentrate on the part of the book with a practical orientation. This is the heart and core of the book and of the method. Didactically seen, the sequence moves from a general focus to particular exercises and procedures, and then back again to a more inclusive level at the end. It is a book that never bores, never preaches, and never drives the reader down one track only. The case examples and graphics consistently deepen and clarify one's understanding of the written text.

One does not have a feeling of having stumbled into a jumbled collection of methods. It is much more the case that the reader can see flexible and varied ways in therapy and counselling to accompany and support a client in the direction of the goal, using various vehicles and various speeds. One can, metaphorically speaking, follow along as a client swims forward in a river, then changes to a car and takes a short cut, and finally, walking along a path and nearing the self-assigned goal, he perhaps pilots down the home stretch in a plane. We have the rewarding experience of seeing how, in this process, the client masters dams in the river, one-way streets, or bad weather fronts, as well as resources. The travellers generally seem to discover these ways themselves and independently open up paths and move closer to their goals.

Above all, one feels the resource- and solution-orientated attitude that respects the clients' autonomy and a basic systemic orientation. To name a few main points, it includes the following: Context sensitivity, circularity of time perspectives, access to a neutral perspective, increasing and decreasing the breadth of focus, moving back and forth between problem and solution (thereby loosening up solutions), anticipating reciprocal effects in a system as a result of a behaviour change of one member, deconstruction, handling ambivalence, and so on.

In view of all the polemic discussion about family constellations, it is a relief to see that it is treated very naturally here as one basic method amongst others. Thereby, the work in family constellations, as developed by Bert Hellinger (Hellinger, Weber a. Beaumont 1998), can be positively enriched by other elements, such as constellations of inner parts of the self, systemic structure constellations (Varga v. Kibéd and Sparrer 2003, Sparrer 2004), or NLP.

The particular strength of this book lies in the orientation towards practice which shows clearly, step-by-step, how, especially in counselling or therapy in an individual setting, various systemic methods and elements can be creatively combined, or used one after another in a series of sessions. These are applicable in the area of personal history, but also in systemically determined patterns. In this regard, this book is an excellent complement to the latest book by Ursula Franke (2003).

The authors themselves clearly state that NIG is not a complete method of psychotherapy in and of itself. When used by experienced practitioners, there is a light, almost playful quality to the descriptions. Anyone planning to use this method, however, should have a solid background and training in one of the acknowledged psychotherapeutic or counselling methods.

Although it may sound contradictory, I would say, at the same time, that readers can experiment themselves with many of the procedures described in this book and achieve positive results.

It is a stimulating and meaningful book that I hope finds many readers.

Gunthard Weber
Wiesloch, July 2003

1. Introduction

Dear Reader,

There is a widespread assumption among fiction writers that a reader participates in the creation of the book, and the form evolves out of a dialogue between the writer and the reader. Although that is mostly a concern of literary convention, the concept is valid in a broader sense. Anyone who has discussed a particular book with a friend is aware that for each person, what is drawn from the book or even read into the book is personal and individual.

In the case of this book, this means that by selecting the chapters that are most pertinent and intriguing to you, you can create a book to be read and used according to your particular preferences. In a comprehensive table of contents and cross-referenced text, we have attempted to create a tool that is workable from any point of entry. Those who lean towards theoretical issues, for example, could start with *"The Existential Paradox"* and the *"Basic Foundation and Principles"*. Those who are more interested in practical applications may want to look at the descriptions of the actual process, and return to the basic explanations later. Others might wish to begin with the chapter on *"Neuro-Imaginative Gestalting"*.

If you are one of those people, as we are, who wants to know who did what in a co-operative effort, Eva Madelung contributed the material that is primarily theoretically orientated, as well as one case study, and Barbara Innecken was responsible primarily for the explanations of process, the applications in practice, and the remaining case studies. There was, naturally, a constant dialogue between us and a reciprocal exchange of ideas and adaptation.

To spare the reader the cumbersome use of multiple pronouns to include males and females, in the discussions we have used masculine and feminine forms alternately. Any imbalance in one direction or the other is unintentional.

Bert Hellinger's Phenomenological Stance: A New Dimension

Bert Hellinger's family constellations were developed as a group therapy form, and the resulting insights have found their way into individual therapy in various ways. This is understandable, since Hellinger's phenomenological stance opens a new dimension in therapy and counselling that has a place in many different approaches.

Compared to the number of books about constellations in groups, by Hellinger himself as well as other colleagues, there has been relatively little written about the potential for this work in an individual setting (cf. Franke 2003; Schneider 1998). This does not correspond to the actual situation, since family constellations are increasingly being included in individual therapy in various forms. The approach and the procedures influence and are included in individual therapy in widely differing ways, and constellations may also be recommended as a complementary adjunct to the on-going therapy process.

Neuro-Imaginative Gestalting as "Open Method"

Neuro-Imaginative Gestalting (NIG), a method developed by Eva Madelung and further developed by Barbara Innecken, combines elements of NLP, brief therapy according to de Shazer, and the Heidelberg School of family therapy, with the family constellation work of Bert Hellinger, and also includes aspects of art therapy and body work. It is a method appropriate to individual therapy and counselling.

NIG is an open rather than self-contained method. Just as it evolved out of the integration of various therapeutic approaches, it may develop further through the reciprocal effects of merging with other methods, thereby stimulating therapeutic creativity. It is only one of many ways of integrating a systemic approach into individual therapy.

In order to work competently, a therapist must have adequate training in another approach to therapy or counselling, sufficient practical experience, and personal awareness and experience. Knowledge of NIG alone is not enough to do therapy or counselling. Anyone choosing to use the NIG approach for their own personal development does so at their own risk.

It is beyond the scope of this book to present the complex approaches that have influenced NIG, as these have been described in detail in other literature. Therefore, we have restricted ourselves to a skeletal presentation of the basic principles and tools in individual therapy.

Prerequisite Knowledge

In order to use NIG in individual or group therapy, in counselling, or as a self-help procedure, a knowledge of NLP is helpful but not absolutely necessary, as the process and effects of working with individual aspects of NIG are described in detail. We consider an understanding of Bert Hellinger's family constellation work important, but it is only absolutely essential as a prerequisite for the element of family constellations in NIG (see p. 86).

We have made every effort to present the background and the procedures in such a way that those trained in the areas mentioned, or in other classical or humanistic methods, can apply this material and gain their own experience and understanding. Each person can then determine whether the information is sufficient or if further training of some kind would be useful.

The Emergence of This Book

Before we turn to the more serious contents of the book, we would like to share with you, our readers, how we found our way to this book, or, how we let ourselves be found.

Barbara Innecken: How I Came to This Book

It must have made quite a picture on a hot summer afternoon in southern Italy: A holiday house by the sea, two children playing on the beach with strict instructions not to go into the water nor into the house. Inside, the father, clad in a bathing suit, is reading aloud to the mother from a book. As the father reads, the mother is busy moving back and forth through the room with papers and pencils and a look of concentration.

What was going on? The book in this true story was Eva Madelung's book on brief therapies, Kurztherapien. Neue Wege zur

Lebensgestaltung [Brief Therapies. New Pathways to Life Gestalting], reading material suggested by Ilse Kutschera and Helmut Eichenmüller, my NLP and family constellations teachers at that time. Both of them were concerned with presenting systemic therapy in a broad context. I had packed the book in my suitcase and found time between beach and pasta to read it. I followed the presentation of the various brief therapies with interest, making a few notes and thinking a bit about it, when suddenly I was wide awake. Under the puzzling title *Neuro-Imaginative Gestalting,* I discovered precise instructions for an exercise that was called *The Life Path* (cf. p. 76). I have always found the long summer holiday, far from the obligations of everyday life, conducive to self-reflection, and this concept spoke to me immediately. I tried to read through the exercise and do it at the same time, which was only moderately successful. So I then asked my husband to lend his assistance, and he patiently accompanied me along the "life path" through an incredible amount of paper.

The Italian meeting with Neuro-Imaginative Gestalting has had a lasting effect. Later, at home, I began using the two exercises described in the brief therapy book in my peer group, in a supervision group, and in my practice. I experimented with ways of integrating them into existing treatment concepts in my psychotherapy and speech therapy practice. At that time, my methodology was based on the applications of kinesiology, systemic psychokinesiology, and, increasingly, family constellations. I quickly discovered that each session took its own particular course, which only partly followed the suggested exercises, an experience that aroused my curiosity. My colleagues, my clients, and myself all shared a similar enthusiasm for the work with NIG, and as far as I could tell in that short time, the effects were also very rewarding and often surprising.

I knew Eva Madelung from our systemic kinesiology group, and at some point I decided to contact her to find out how I could learn more about NIG. She suggested that I come into her practice and learn more NIG exercises through personal experience and supervision; an offer I was happy to accept. Eva was a calm and sensitive guide who never interfered, but also never wavered. In that setting, the personal and professional experience I developed went far beyond learning a few exercises. To give you an impression of my experience, I have described my first session in NIG, "the two trees", in the last chapter of this book.

The end of the story is quickly told. At some point I asked Eva why she didn't publish this practical and valuable method in a book. She said she didn't want to write any more professional books. On the one hand, of course, I respected this position, but on the other hand, I couldn't let go of the idea of a book about Neuro-Imaginative Gestalting. Since I had had some experience with writing myself, I cautiously asked Eva if she would consider writing this book with me. The answer to my question did not come for some months, but when it did, it was a firm yes.

The results of our co-operative efforts are now in your hands, dear reader, and we hope that you will discover something in it that serves as a stimulus for you, and perhaps accompanies you for a while on your own personal and professional path.

Eva Madelung: How This Book Came to Me

Years ago when I wrote the book *Kurztherapien. Neue Wege zur Lebens-gestaltung* (Madelung 1996), I had intended to complete it with a practical book in which the abbreviated description of NIG would be described in detail. However, when the book was finished, this idea faded as other plans took its place. I didn't really think any more about actually doing it, even though I got a lot of positive feedback from colleagues who learned the method in my training groups.

From time to time, various colleagues who were already working with NIG came to me asking for supervision. In fact, it was just such a request that brought Barbara Innecken to my practice. As she has described above, she had already been applying what was presented in the brief therapy book. Since I was no longer offering training by that time, she opted to learn more through personal experience and supervision.

I was astounded when, after a time, she asked if I would write a book about this method. Following my initial refusal, she came back with the idea of writing a practical book co-operatively with her. Although I felt pleased about her offer and the recognition implicit in it, I still hesitated because I had plans for a different project. There was, however, some material from my training programme that I put at Barbara's disposal. From this material she came up with a lay-out, and I was hooked.

I am now very thankful to Barbara for taking the initiative. Without her competent work this book would never have come to fruition. I hope that it provides a therapeutic stimulus for the readers and rouses a few new thoughts. It is a summary of my therapeutic work, and in the conclusion, I have included a few references to my own personal experience and the understanding I have reached through this work.

2. Neuro-Imaginative Gestalting (NIG)

DESCRIPTION

In the early nineties, I attended many training seminars with Robert Dilts, who, together with Richard Bandler and John Grinder, belonged to the first generation of Neuro-Linguistic Programming (NLP). I learned some essentials with Dilts which later, from my own practice and in combination with other methods, I developed further into Neuro-Imaginative Gestalting.

The name "Neuro-Imaginative Gestalting" is an indication that this method is a variation of Neuro-Linguistic Programming. The word "neuro" refers to the fact that proceeding in this way with inner images has to do with neuro-psychologically conditioned effects, just as is true in NLP.

Substituting "imaginative" for "linguistic" was prompted because in NLP, a major consideration is the attention to language as the tool of expression, and here the attention is shifted to expression through the creation of images. In NLP, ideas are described in words. In NIG, in addition to the linguistic description, we have a pictorial representation. What the two methods have in common is an awareness of unconscious body signals. In NIG there is also a focus on the unconscious signals included in the pictorial representation (cf. p. 61).

Replacing the term "programming" with "gestalting" was particularly important for me, because I have never really felt comfortable with the programming metaphor, which in any case only represents a half-truth (cf. p. 27). It implies that the human brain is "conditioned" completely from the outside, and that a therapist can programme a client for health without the individual's participation.

From what I have personally experienced and in my practice, the metaphor of an inner artist who uses inner and external conditions to permit the emergence of an appropriate pattern of living seems to me to be more suitable. Therefore, the term "life gestalting" was particularly close to my heart, as expressed in the sub-title of my book *Kurztherapien. Neue Wege zur Lebensgestaltung.* Additionally, I wanted to set myself apart from the emphasis on "personal power" that is so prominently represented by some NLP trainers and clients. That approach, in which a goal, independent of content and the effects of the environment, can supposedly be created when visualized in the proper way, is non-systemic in my opinion. Even when it is successful, which may happen in some cases, it does not generally lead to a lasting solution if other aspects are simply excluded.

I must add, however, that in no way are all NLP trainers proponents of this one-sided approach. With Robert Dilts, one can learn an NLP approach that in many ways relies on a context orientation.

THE DEVELOPMENT OF NIG FROM PRACTICE

As described in my brief therapy book, NIG was developed in several stages. The first experience was a therapy with a suicidal client for whom painting was the most important tool of expression and eventually became a resource.

Then the work with floor anchors with Robert Dilts was added. In this method, the images relevant to the therapy, such as the image of a goal, the image of the present with its problems, or the images of resources, are not only described verbally and anchored with touch, as is generally the case in NLP, but are described verbally and then with the help of sheets of typing paper they are laid out on the floor. In this way, the client can physically move back and forth between the images. In doing so, the body is incorporated as a "source of intuition" (cf. p. 40).

In my practice this quickly led to the use of symbols such as stones, seeds, and coloured felt squares instead of blank papers. In a demonstration of work with a "life path" in a group, sketches were added to the blank papers. This idea arose out of the situation at that time, and had positive effects that convinced me to adopt the self-creation of spatial anchors in my individual practice.

Laying out self-created images or coloured felt squares also proved useful in doing family constellations in individual therapy, whereas up to this time I had used pillows for this purpose. The concrete process of entering into the inner images and moving between them made a more authentic feedback possible, coupled with a precise awareness of physical reactions.

NIG as Systemic Therapy

The essential characteristic of systemic therapies is the fact that here it is not the individual who commands attention in the foreground, but rather the relationship connections. A person is always seen as a part of his family or a general human relationship system. This is called "context orientation".

The Reciprocal Effects of Perception, Inner Images, Feeling, Representation, Action, and Environment

A part of the systemic viewpoint comes from an observation of quantum physics that the observer and the observed have reciprocal effects, and therefore, there is no objective reality independent from the observer.

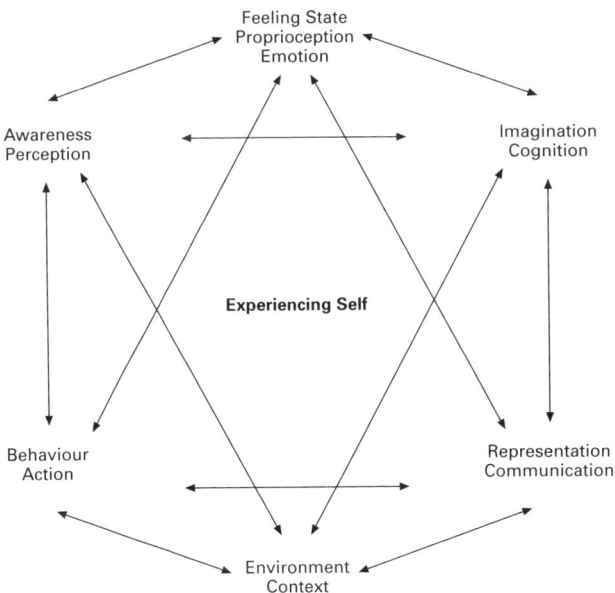

Diagram: Model of the reality of reciprocal effects

My brief therapy book already includes this model of the reality of reciprocal effects in which the circular triad of perception, inner images, and feeling is the most important element, and is connected to a similarly reciprocal triad of representation, action, and environment (Madelung 1996).

This means: What people experience as real is not objective reality. A construct of reality always occurs in the reciprocal effects between various aspects. That is, it is always a co-construction in relationship with others from inside and outside the family. The systemic and constructivist viewpoints are closely related.

Using this model, you can also see which point in the reciprocal system you are working on therapeutically at any given moment. For example, if a sketch of an inner image is representative of communication, in the lower right hand corner, the process of sketching affects the inner image and at the same time alters the perception of the situation and possibly also the feeling state. According to the schema, regardless of where you intervene, the entire system of relationship is set in motion, with a resulting change in the whole.

From the underlying basis of this model, it is also clear that NIG is systemic in the multiple reciprocal effects of all components. By creating images and through the physical act of laying them out and stepping into them, the client experiences that certain images have an effect on feelings and her state of being. On the other hand, she experiences, through body awareness, the effects of the representation on the original image, which again has an effect on the feeling state and vice versa. In this way, in a circular interplay between the elements of reality, a psychic reality is constructed which can have a positive, lasting influence on her outlook on life and how she feels.

INCORPORATING FAMILY CONSTELLATIONS

As mentioned above, NLP often pays little or no attention to relationship connections. Incorporating family constellations in NIG addresses this deficit. One learns not only to look at life's circumstances from different angles in order to find resolutions, but also to look through the eyes of another (cf. p. 51). The dimension of the basic orders of relationships (cf. p. 45) is also brought into the process.

NIG as an Integration of Constructivist and Phenomenological Approaches

In NIG we assume that the systemic-constructivist approach and the systemic-phenomenological approach are both justifiable. Both correspond to our life experience of our own psychic reality (cf. p. 29). The created reality of the constructivist approach is complemented by the manifested reality of the phenomenological approach of Bert Hellinger. This weaves a metaphor of our experience of life and the world that corresponds more closely to reality than is the case when only one of these aspects is acknowledged. Therefore, a basic principle of NIG is to take both of these approaches into consideration.

The Element of Art Therapy

The American ethnologist and philosopher, Gregory Bateson, suggested that artistic endeavours can provide a creative response to double bind situations (Bateson 1972). There are actually artists who, in psychotic like states, have been able to help themselves through their artistic expression.

In the sixties and seventies, as systemic therapy was being developed in the USA, there was also movement in the art scene. John Cage, for example, said, "Art is a kind of research laboratory in which you try out life. You don't stop living while you're busy creating art, and when you live ... you don't stop creating art." (Cage 1991). Predominant at that time was a search for a direct connection between art and life. "(Art) is concerned with changes in the habits of hearing and seeing, and the mind", said Cage (1991), and identified one of the most important instruments of systemic therapy, the change of viewpoint, that is, re-framing.

In Germany, Joseph Beuys repeatedly emphasized the life-shaping and therapeutic aspects of modern art. This was convincingly summarized and presented by Gertraud Schottenloher who, among other things, maintained that the "actual goal of therapy, the shaping of self and life, was closely connected to art in ancient times" (Schottenloher and Schnell 1994, p.17). Considering the direct connection to life modern art often strives for, it appears appropriate today to include artistic creation in therapeutic procedures. Along with art therapy, we have music therapy, dance therapy, creative writing, and so on. The question always comes up in discussion whether psychotherapy isn't closer to an art than to a science, an idea I think is worthy of consideration.

DISTINGUISHING NIG FROM ART THERAPY

NIG is a "psychotherapy with art components", as Schottenloher rightfully distinguishes it from actual art therapy (Schottenloher and Schnell). "Working on a picture", and the artistic process that plays a central role in art therapy, is replaced here with "working with the picture" in the systemic sense. This "working with the picture" includes a spatial arrangement of pictures, physical movement, and attention to body awareness in the therapeutic process.

NIG is a way for therapists who work systemically to enrich their work with creative elements, lending a particular quality of self-awareness. The client has to feel completely free from any artistic expectations. That also means that he is free to choose whether he completes a detailed sketch or just a symbol on the paper (for example, a letter, a number, or a word). He decides himself whether his sketch will be abstract, objective, or something else.

Despite, or perhaps because of, this freedom, the result is often impressive images that remain with their creator for a long time as resource anchors, regardless of whether they are aesthetically pleasing or not.

Schottenloher sets forth basic principles for art therapy practiced by artists that are remarkably similar to the procedures in systemic work. In addition to self-regulation, they include a solution orientation, "re-framing", and the "construction of new realities" (Schottenloher and Schnell 1994).

These common features are an indication of the common features between creative therapy procedures and systemic therapy procedures. Both approaches endeavour to establish a connection to the unknowable unconscious, which is actively shaping us from within, and between us all in order to fulfil life. What matters is protecting, strengthening, and caring for this connection.

THE ELEMENT OF BODY THERAPY

We have already mentioned that an awareness of body sensations is one of the most important instruments of NIG. Family constellations are also similarly dependent upon an awareness of physical reactions and impulses. It is important to distinguish clearly between physical feelings and emotional feelings, although the two are closely related.

By focusing on the physical sensations in response to various positions, the body becomes a source of intuition about possible solutions. A discharge of feelings should not generally be encouraged and allowed only in so far as absolutely necessary. Therefore, body work methods that rely on concentration are more similar to NIG than methods that encourage letting out or discharging emotions.

Seen practically, a centring exercise taken from breathing therapy, for example, would be more useful as a preparation for this work than a discharging bio-energetic exercise.

3. Basic Principles and Assumptions

PREFACE

In the following chapters, *"Basic Principles and Assumptions"* and *"Tools of NIG"*, it has not always been possible to make clear subdivisions. There is also some overlap between the chapters *"Tools of NIG"* and *"Procedures"*. For the sake of clarity, we have included the subdivisions anyway and the detailed table of contents will help in cases of doubt.

Some of the basic principles and assumptions have been drawn from NLP and others from Hellinger's family constellations. The complementary effect of the two together is specific to NIG. What has been drawn from NLP is in the first section, and the assumptions drawn from family constellations are presented in the section after *"Handling Feelings in NIG"*.

"ENTERING THE IMAGE":
THINKING IN IMAGES BETWEEN AWARENESS AND MOVEMENT

As described in the chapter *"Neuro-Imaginative Gestalting"*, the therapeutic effectiveness of NIG rests on the reciprocal effects of imaging, representation, awareness, feelings, action, and environment. Clients are always amazed at the variety of bodily sensations that arise when they put themselves into their own inner images; this means physically standing on their sketches in the various chosen positions. Since pictures express more than words are able to capture and describe, and the reaction of the body occurs unconsciously, a "dialogue with the unconscious" (Robert Dilts) is made possible. The images represented are experienced on the one hand as messages *from* the unconscious, and on the other hand they have the effect of a message *to* the

26

unconscious (cf. p. 37). The pictorial representation does justice to the language of the unconscious in a way that verbal language cannot.

The concrete, physical "entering into" the sphere of the picture results in a coupling of visual images and body awareness, and a synthesis of visual and kinaesthetic areas (cf. p. 40) emerges. This means that out of the visual awareness, a physical state develops that has a reflecting effect on the awareness and also with the other components that are connected in the "reciprocal reality". You can experience in your own body how your imagination creates feelings and sensations and thus influences how you feel and consequently what you imagine.

In addition, this process provides an experience of the fact that thinking is linked to movement and movement is connected to awareness in a reciprocal way.

Through Neuro-Imaginative Gestalting, you can experience, therefore, that imaginative thinking is a mental capability that provides a necessary complement to logical thinking, particularly in psychological areas.

Gestalting Instead of Programming

NLP uses the metaphor of programming for the therapeutic process, in which changes are effected through the influence of another person while the recipient remains passive. Whether, and to what extent the brain is like a computer that can be programmed and reprogrammed as this metaphor implies, is a questionable issue for cognitive research. In the end, everyone more or less agrees that this model falls short of reality. After all, the real human brain is the creator of the real computer; the computer did not create the human brain, even though its structure partially reflects a cognitive process.

In NIG, the programming metaphor is replaced by the metaphor of creative shaping, and the image of a programmer by one of an inner artist. A personally shaped image used as an anchor is qualitatively different from the usual anchors of touch used in NLP. Through sketches, positioning, and feeling, the client experiences himself not as an "object of re-programming", but as someone shaping and forming himself. This shaping is a dialogue between conscious and unconscious aspects which occurs in every creative process. In this shaping, the unconscious part cannot be given orders; it has to be met with respect. This reflects the paradoxical or complementary relationship that determines our lives right down to the everyday details, the relationship between opportunities for forming ourselves and being at the mercy of external givens (cf. p. 183). Even a great artist can never achieve a comprehensive reproduction of his inner vision with the materials at hand. He is restricted to those materials.

REALITY OF RECIPROCAL EFFECTS AS A METAPHOR OF CONTEXT ORIENTATION

In the chapter *"Neuro-Imaginative Gestalting"* (cf. p. 19), we have met the concept of a reality of reciprocal effects. Circular thinking, which corresponds to this model, departs from the thought patterns of linear causality. This means that the usual thought pattern of cause and effect, in which the first event determines the second, is replaced by a thought structure of relationship, in which the effects have a retroactive effect on the causes. In this way, systemic thought is always circular and context orientated.

RECIPROCAL EFFECTS OF PAST, PRESENT, AND FUTURE IN LIFE PATHS AND RE-IMPRINTING

The NIG element of "re-imprinting" (cf. p. 97), like the work with life paths (cf. p. 76), at first sight looks like a linear, causal biography: From the present with its problems, you go back into the past to find causes in the form of negative beliefs and to look for positive resources. The process becomes circular when the perspective from a goal or an image of resolution is included. By looking at the present situation through the eyes of the future person, standing in the resolved situation in the future, there is an effect on the present. The present is changed as the person becomes aware of new possibilities for resolution from a different perspective. From this point, the past can also be looked at differently. Crises or problematic phases can be seen in relation to the whole, and therefore, differently. Returning to the present from a place of resolution in the future, the awareness of the past is different and the present has also changed. In this way, the wheel of time perspective begins to turn the reciprocity of influence in a back and forth movement between the positions. This continues until an adequate choice of possibilities for resolution is at hand and the process comes to a resting place.

Reality of Reciprocal Effects of the NIG Elements "Two Sides"

In the NIG element "two sides" (cf. p. 106), the reality of reciprocal effects is experienced at close range. In sketching the images, situations are seen and represented from more than one side. By moving back and forth between the poles, the reciprocal influences can be felt physically. Normally, a synthesis of the two viewpoints emerges that opens up opportunities for resolution. This experience can be seen as an advanced level of imaginative conceptualization.

Reciprocity Between the Biographical Level and the Level of the Orders of Relationship

At the biographical level lie our personal experiences with people and places we know and the circumstances we were born into. This view of the biographical level shares common features with not only the systemic-constructivist viewpoint, but also with humanistic, behavioural, and analytic approaches. At this level, depending on the method, we are looking at drives, bonds, dreams, complexes, transference, conditioning, blocks, peak experiences, delegations, resources, or beliefs.

On the level of the orders of relationships, on the other hand, we have access to the effects of the extended family relationships that may have resulted in entanglements. In this regard, we include even those individuals who are unknown, or who perhaps had some exceptional fate, or events from long ago that have affected the whole family. For example, the fate of an uncle who was killed in the war may have an effect on his nephew's life, even though they may not have known one another.

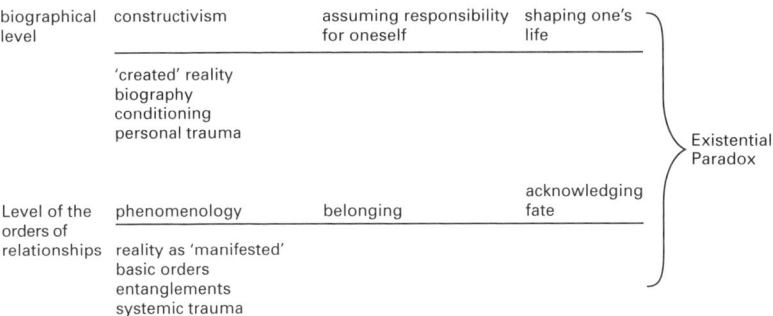

biographical level	constructivism	assuming responsibility for oneself	shaping one's life	Existential Paradox
	'created' reality biography conditioning personal trauma			
Level of the orders of relationships	phenomenology	belonging	acknowledging fate	
	reality as 'manifested' basic orders entanglements systemic trauma			

Diagram: Model of Interactive Levels

These two levels interact, each affecting the other, and it is advisable to find a way to include both in the therapeutic process, as is done in NIG.

Writing about learning to lead family constellations, Bert Hellinger reports the words of a course participant, "In NLP you learn how to swim. If you have a heavy stone hung round your neck, then you sink even if you know how to swim. If you get rid of the stone, for example through a family constellation, you still have to learn to swim" (Hellinger 2002a). The reference to NLP is also true for many other approaches that are designed to help someone "learn to swim". The most common of these have been mentioned above.

The Model of Interactive Levels as a Basic Metaphor of NIG

The model of levels shows that when using those NIG elements taken from NLP, the work is at the biographical level and has to do with the client's personal experiences and beliefs formed through those experiences. In the NLP style, the therapeutic process consists of dissolving old, negative beliefs (for example, "I can't expose myself as I really am") by looking at them in a different light and replacing them with positive beliefs appropriate to the current situation.

However, if, for example, the father of a family has seemingly appropriate goals – perhaps reducing his debts and achieving financial independence – but unconsciously keeps sabotaging himself, you might suspect that an entanglement at the level of the orders of relationships is preventing resolution at the biographical level. Therefore, it is useful to check whether there might be something in the system, perhaps an identification with another family member who was unable to face some personal guilt. An entanglement like that might impel a descendent to unconsciously step into that position and punish himself in some way (cf. p. 44). The situation can be clarified using sketches or symbols, or a family constellation in a group.

The Inner and External Family

We can call the inner parts of the self that we work with in NIG the "inner family". We see again and again that there is an interactive, reciprocal relationship between this inner family and the external family, our family of origin. If you relate this aspect to the model of interactive levels, the inner family is located at the biographical level, and the external family at the level of the order of relationships. The inner family and the external family are interactive in their effects in the same way as the two levels in the model.

The Model of Levels: Supporting the Client's Understanding

Looking at an image of resolution in a constellation with representatives, or working with a family image (cf. p. 86), many clients are prone to say, "How lovely, if it had only been like that. But it wasn't!" Most have a better understanding if you explain that the level of the orders of relationships may be different to the biographical reality, and that a resolution at this level lies in acknowledging the basic orders (cf. p. 45). You might make a comment such as, "This configuration you have laid out here is a reality that comes out of personal experiences in this family. There is, however, an underlying reality that is somewhat different and more consequential. There is a father, a mother, their children, and other family members, and that structure of relationship has a certain order that has an effect on everyone whether they know about it and acknowledge it or not."

A Change of Viewpoint

"Changing the viewpoint" is an essential element of systemic therapy. It comes from a context orientation that focuses on relationship connections rather than on the personal fate of one individual. We have already mentioned (cf. p. 21) that our world is constructed from interactive influences. This necessitates looking at it from more than one point of view. Different people will see a situation differently, and we can even see our own situation differently from various viewpoints within ourselves.

When we include these different perspectives, potential resolutions appear that would not otherwise be thought of. A change of perspective is, therefore, one of the most important tools in proceeding systemically.

Resolution and Resource Orientation

All systemic therapies are orientated towards resolution and resources. This means that we attend less to the deficits and traumas of the past than to the task of bringing forth possibilities for resolutions and sources of strength. The importance of this is clear when we consider how much stronger the motivation, and therefore the energy is for a person who has an appropriate goal in mind as opposed to someone who is primarily concerned with looking for the cause of current problems. Together with the above-mentioned context-orientation, this is the essential differing factor between systemic therapies and psychoanalysis.

GOALS AND RESOLUTIONS

Although these two concepts overlap and are sometimes used as synonyms, it is important to distinguish between them.

An inappropriate goal does not offer resolution in a problem situation (cf. p. 78). Usually, it has no impact at all, but it might make a problem worse or even cause lasting damage. On the other hand, it is often difficult to distinguish an appropriate goal from an inappropriate one, and there are cases where despite (or perhaps due to) a goal that appears impossible, something amazing is accomplished.

Particularly in the work with life paths, it is important to pay close attention to the appropriateness of the concept of goal. If that is done, the goal concept becomes a resource that helps in taking the next step.

In family constellations, however, an imagined goal is not a consideration. A resolution emerges through the acknowledgement of the basic orders or the "movements of the soul" (cf. p. 45 and Hellinger 2002a). In any event, the goal is usually voiced in the client's statement of the issue.

If we look at ourselves and others, it is clear that we almost always have some image of our future, perhaps only unconsciously, and perhaps nothing more than a desire to go on living. Pictures of the future, negative or positive, arise spontaneously in our minds in the form of sometimes very brief daydreams that suddenly appear out of the unconscious, fed by memories and fantasies, and against which we are powerless. Even consciously chosen appropriate goals may be dimmed or obliterated by anxieties about the future that can sap or completely drain our life energy.

The Concept of the Goal as a Basic Internal Image

In therapy or counselling, the image of a goal is as important as an image of the client's family. Both are basic images that affect us, regardless of any awareness of them. An appropriate concept of the goal is a source of strength, just as an image of the family is a resource at the level of the basic orders. An image of one's family in harmony with the natural orders is, however, the more powerful resource of the two.

Context Orientation of a Concept of Goals

Those who have learned to think systemically know that a resolution must be an outcome that is good for everyone. In this light, we have to consider whether the achievement of a goal will also serve others, or at least not be harmful to them. This is an aspect of family constellations that is incorporated into NIG, whereas it is often ignored in NLP.

Achievement of Goals Is Not Really in Our Hands

When a goal has been reached, we can look back and analyse what contributed effectively to this achievement. We can see that in the end, it is always dependent on a systemic influence. For example, a case of the flu could have prevented someone from being present for an examination. Or, certain questions in an exam might have kept the person from achieving the mark needed. Or, or, or … in the end, we are always tied to a network of related people and events.

Goals Are "Attractors" (Robert Dilts)

"Attractors" are sources of strength in the future that draw us forward and activate and concentrate our life energies. They usually work best when they are not too precise, and remain somewhat vague. Then, the unconscious, or what we might even call a co-conscious (see below), can modify and transform. It often happens that a person breaks loose and ends up in a different place, or perhaps comes back to an old goal in a new form via a roundabout way (for example, a professional goal from one's youth). In a personal growth group, as we talked about goals, a young girl said, "In my experience, the things I particularly long for are the things I don't get". We should try to distinguish between appropriate goals and longings. The problem is, that it is only in hindsight that we know whether an image of a goal was helpful in some way, even if it was not completely realized, or whether it turned out to be completely unrealistic or a dead end.

On the other hand, there is the supposition, based on experience, that a concept of the goal should be formulated as precisely as possible and be present through all the senses if it is to have any chance of realization. In this context, the founders of NLP are of two minds: Bandler encourages a precise formulation, Grinder prefers a vague goal.

The Path as the Goal

On the one hand, it makes sense to concern ourselves with a concept of the goal and include that in our decision-making and problem solving. In addition to the energy that well-chosen goals provide, our psyches are apparently so constructed that, consciously or unconsciously, we carry images of our goals, even if it is only the goal to be free to stay in the "here and now".

On the other hand, with observation, the sense of being the "doer" dissolves and we begin to ask ourselves if the goal was really so important, and who was it exactly that achieved this goal? To use a now well-worn phrase, wasn't "the path actually the goal?"

Such questions lead us into a spiritual arena, but need not hinder us from accepting, with relief and gratitude, a solution that may have emerged.

The State of Needing No More Advice (de Shazer)

In NIG it is useful to formulate goal concepts with de Shazer's orientation: Imagine yourself in a state in the future where you do not need any advice. This means a point at which everything that seems like a problem now has either disappeared or has been changed in a way that makes it possible for you to deal with it. In this way, from the very beginning, the focus is on possible solutions. At the same time, it implies that clients, given the right conditions, can or must learn to deal with problems themselves, for example, simply by avoiding certain situations. Additionally, this formulation of the question prevents setting goals too high or too unrealistically.

OTHER RESOURCES

Other sources of strength are, for example, memories of difficult situations in the past that were dealt with well. They remind the unconscious of potential creative abilities. "That time you were able to find a solution, so you can do it now, too." Memories of sensory experiences of natural beauty, or strongly aesthetic or spiritual experiences also serve as sources of strength.

RESOURCES, DEFICITS, AND TRAUMAS

No one would argue with the fact that there have been severe traumas and deficits in some personal histories, and they must be included, directly or indirectly, within the framework of a therapy. In Steve de Shazer's radically solution-oriented approach, one does not ask about the problem nor about its supposed or actual cause, but enquires rather about when things are or were better.

In NLP, "re-imprinting" is a therapeutic element used in working with traumas (cf. p. 97). Using the NIG element of "two sides", (cf. p. 106) may reveal traumatized aspects of the person.

SYSTEMIC BOND TRAUMA (FRANZ RUPPERT)

In his book, *Verwirrte Seelen* [Disturbed Souls], Franz Ruppert talks about traumas to systemic bonds (Ruppert 2002). He is referring to events that affect a family so strongly that they are passed on as entanglements through the following generations. This means that linear causality has to be taken into consideration. Different approaches deal with this issue in different ways. In therapy approaches based on a problem orientation – for example, psychoanalysis – we look at early childhood trauma as the cause of current problem situations. In systemic therapies, focused on solutions, we seek inner images that provide a picture of resolution and try to activate sources of strength.

CAUSES ARE CONVICTIONS, NOT FACTS (ROBERT DILTS)

This formulation in reference to psychological connections challenges the kind of problem orientated, linear thinking that looks back at causes. Even though childhood experiences undoubtedly have an impact and can severely damage an individual, we still have to ask whether some particular behaviour of the person's mother or father is really the only cause of the current problems. If so, it would follow that the parents are to blame for the present difficulty. It may be tempting to regard the situation this way, but our experience has been that it is minimally helpful, if at all, and then only briefly.

Certainly in less dramatic cases, where no real trauma appears to have been the cause of the problem, we should ask whether it is not more reasonable to look at the network of connections as multi-causal, influenced by more than one cause, or even better, circular-causal, that is, connected through reciprocal interaction. It is always an open question whether the assertion of a linear, causal relationship really reflects the reality of the situation or whether it reflects only the structure of what we are able to recognize.

When intense reactions are involved, such as being justifiably angry with someone because they have treated us badly or hurt us, it is difficult to look for the circular-causality. Still, an attempt is worth the effort because if successful, a resolution usually emerges or, if it is an issue concerning a parent, it may be possible to let go in a good way.

PSYCHO-AESTHETICS AND PSYCHO-GEOGRAPHY (ROBERT DILTS)

The term "psycho-aesthetics" identifies an ability to imagine and depict inner states and pictures. Without this capability, NIG would not be possible. This is an experience of a living metaphor of our life creativity. We do not know how we actually know when one sketch and its position are precisely right and another is not, but clients almost always have a very clear sense about it. Initially, the task of representing a specific image seems impossible, often because it is not very specific. Still, in some inexplicable way, a representation usually emerges with an amazing inner logic and meaning.

The term "psycho-geography" refers to the map of images that results in laying the sketches out on the floor. The positions in space become a metaphor for inner relationships; positions are coupled to physical and emotional states.

MESSAGES TO THE UNCONSCIOUS

Systemic therapies make use of the fact that the unconscious not only sends messages, but also receives them.

Pictures of resources may be remembered or referred to in problem situations to aid in the search for solutions. The unconscious is reminded of previous avenues leading to solutions. The exercise of retrieving resources from the life path is based upon this experience. The fact that a person's unconscious can be influenced has long been known. It usually occurs in situations having to do with suggestions, for example, the influence of advertising or political propaganda. If this influence were not effective, millions would not be spent on it each year. An even more extreme example of this phenomenon is hypnosis, in which a person's unconscious is given instructions. The French psychiatrist Charcot employed this technique, among others, to cure hysteria, which was widespread in the nineteenth century, and Freud learned it from him. He discovered, however, that the cure was not always successful, and direct hypnosis disappeared from the development of psychoanalysis. It was replaced by dream interpretation, which found meaning in the messages sent from the unconscious in dreams. The biblical story of Joseph is an indication that this was not a new idea either.

INDIRECT SUGGESTION AND DIALOGUE WITH THE UNCONSCIOUS

The American psychiatrist, Milton H. Erickson, studied psychoanalysis as well as classic hypnosis, as was common in the United States. He honed the skill of trance induction to the level of a virtuoso and became a master at sending messages *to* the unconscious, calling this process "indirect suggestion". He had decided that Freud's concept of "resistance" was correct, and that direct hypnosis was often unsuccessful in the long-term. In his experience, the unconscious does not respond well to being forced; it is more effective to present a selection of various possible solutions from which the unconscious can freely choose the most suitable. When his patients were in a slightly altered state of consciousness, he told them various stories that he regarded as suitable, and which carried embedded possible solutions. He was extremely successful with these "indirect suggestions". Countless students have learned this method from him, and it is used not only in Ericksonian hypnotherapy, but also explicitly or implicitly in NLP and other systemic methods.

In NIG, we can assume that merely sketching inner images puts a person in a mild state of trance, as this is what occurs in any situation in which someone turns their focus inward. A formal trance induction is unnecessary. The concentration and physical sensations that develop as someone stands and moves amongst the sheets of paper have the effect of deepening this trance-like state. It can usually be felt in the increasing stillness or density in the room. A "dialogue with the unconscious" (R. Dilts) results from the experience of being physically in the metaphors, the physical act of standing on the images and moving about (cf. p. 52). This "living metaphor" is combined with the visual impact of the pictures that contain positive suggestions from the unconscious. The messages *from* the unconscious revealed through the pictorial expression and in the physical sensations interact with messages *to* the unconscious in the form of images of resources and the "living metaphors" described above. The conscious mind is only partially involved in this process. Healing occurs even when we are not consciously aware of the details of the process and cannot understand them. The oft-quoted phrase from Milton Erickson, "The unconscious mind is so much wiser than the conscious mind" led him to believe that it was better if a client could completely forget the contents of a session, so that his conscious mind would not interfere with the integrative activity of the unconscious mind. In a similar way, Bert Hellinger has recommended that clients forget the results of a constellation so that the experience can continue to have effects in the unconscious without disturbance.

Today, Erickson's students, such as Ernest Rossi and Stephen Gilligan, as well as NLP practitioners, consider the above-mentioned concept of a "dialogue with the unconscious" to be a process that takes place on the razor-thin edge between conscious and unconscious, moving back and forth between the two.

The Image is the Message

In the chapter *"Neuro-Imaginative Gestalting"*, we have already described how the pictorial images and the use of such images as "spatial anchors" were developed out of a demonstration (cf. p. 20). As I observed the effects of this process while using various elements of NLP in individual therapy, I slowly became aware of the possibilities at hand.

We can consider the images to be effective elements, which in NLP the client is asked to describe in language. The representation of inner images offers additional information to the therapist as well as the client. Above all, when the non-dominant hand is used, the representations make statements that are often very surprising. Unconscious aspects are revealed and the therapist can make suggestions that would be impossible in a purely linguistic communication. The client can also often see aspects clearly and directly which were previously unconscious. Pictures say, if not more, then something different from words. The total impression is often what makes the difference and what remains in memory for a long time.

REAL OR UNREAL?

Bert Hellinger makes a distinction between an inner image and reality. He places inner images in the sphere of fantasy and imagination. In this he distinguishes his phenomenologically orientated methods from those with a constructivist orientation. In his view, constructs are unreal because they are imagined; phenomena are real because they can be experienced.

On the other hand, he often calls up his own inner images to explain his interventions and these images frequently reflect the client's psychological reality. He also sometimes suggests that a client simply hold an image of the resolved state in harmony with the orders of relationship and allow this image to have its effect, and to hold back on any intentional change of behaviour. This means that even for him, certain images have an effect on the psyche and are part of the reality of relationships. His first request of every client is to set up a constellation of the relationships according to an inner picture. This would not be permissible, and the work would have no effect, if the image of the relationships were a mere construct. Imagination and awareness interact with each other.

In NIG, this corresponds to the need to determine whether a goal image is an appropriate one or whether it has to do with unreal wishes and longings (for example, in work with the "life path" element) (cf. p. 78). There are fantasy images that are ungrounded and cut off from an awareness of self and others. They either have no effect or they may turn out to be destructive. In an individual setting, you usually get some feeling about whether you and the client are moving in the realm of pure fantasy or in the realm of the soul's reality, but, of course, one is never fully immune to error. If anything can be counted on for surprises, it is surely the soul.

The concrete translation of inner image to pictorial representation in NIG is a way of learning to handle inner images respectfully.

Synaesthesia, Interactive Sensory Experience

We are accustomed to speaking of melodies as sweet or bitter, or of sounds as hard or soft. These are metaphors of speech that indicate that the areas of sensation mix with one another. For some people it is quite extreme, and for them, certain tones, tone combinations, or even numbers, are always associated with particular colours. For others, certain physical sensations are connected to tones. Seeing, hearing, feeling, smelling, and tasting are apparently not clearly delineated at the level of neurons. Synaesthesia accounts for the experience that a configuration of images is connected to physical sensations and emotions for the person standing on the images.

The Physical Body as a Source of Intuition and as Sensor

In bio-energetics, the body is seen as memories made flesh. Physical release serves both to reveal and to work through traumatic memories. In systemic processes, physical symptoms are regarded as messages within the system from the mind, body, and spirit.

We know that the body can be a source of intuition based on everyday experiences, of "a gut reaction to" or "feeling for" something that leads us towards solutions. As Gernot Böhme says, the body is the part of nature that we ourselves are. The body is a "partner with non-negotiable conditions" (Gunther Schmidt). In one sense it is a limiting factor, but on the other hand, it often has wisdom beyond that of our understanding; wisdom that is very close to the wisdom of the unconscious.

The focus on physical awareness plays a critical role in NIG. A client who can really enter into this process is put into the light trance needed for the process of change. The physical body becomes a source of intuition about possible solutions and a sensor for the various qualities of images, for example, if a goal is appropriate, or if a position in the family system feels right or not.

Organization of the Self in Dialogue with the Unconscious

As previously mentioned, a continuous "dialogue with the unconscious" occurs in NIG through the work with images created spontaneously with the non-dominant hand, and the inclusion of the physical experience of various positions. When a client depicts a problem or a person in a sketch, it makes a statement. The unintentional elements that enter into the image have a reciprocal effect on the client. Looking at the sketch, things are now visible that were not noticed previously. By talking over these reactions with the therapist, the observations have a reciprocal, dialogic effect with the feedback from the therapist. The therapist can both look through the lens of the image, and also provide a different point of view drawn from experience and intuition. This dialogic, reciprocal process continues as the client stands on the various sheets of paper and attends to the involuntary physical reactions that occur. Precise observations on the part of the therapist intensify the interactive process.

In this way, the therapist can remain in the background for much of the time, adopting the role of an assistant who hands over appropriate tools when needed, and leaving room for the wisdom of the unconscious. Time and again, one stands amazed at this unrelenting and effective process, qualities that also make this procedure appropriate for self-help (cf. p. 127).

The above refers mostly to the elements taken from NLP. Family constellations in individual work require an outside observer-helper.

Feelings in NIG

"Love is part of the order. Order comes before love, and love can only develop within the framework of order" (Hellinger, Weber a. Beaumont 2001). This statement refers to primary love as the basic emotion in family relationships, but also more generally means that emotions can have a healing effect only within the natural orders of relationships. This decisively distinguishes the systemic-phenomenological viewpoint from the feeling-orientated viewpoint of humanistic approaches such as primal therapy or bio-energetics, in which the expression of a flow of emotion is regarded as the primary factor in healing.

It is particularly important in work with family constellations to discriminate between primary feelings, secondary feelings, and feelings taken over from another person.

Primary feelings arise directly out of a situation and are usually strong but brief. Others can sympathize with these feelings.

In constellation work, primary love is the most essential feeling. We can see how archaic and vital this power is by the fact that we share it with other mammals that are also born with an instinct for caring for their young. Primary love is a drive and therefore blind. It ensures that humans can grow up protected within a family. On the other hand, it lies behind every entanglement, causing violations of the orders of family relationships, driven by love. A frequently cited example is a child bonded through love, unconsciously taking on guilt that belongs to a parent, and in doing so, causing harm to himself and to his parents. Primary love also lies behind the hate and conflict that rule in some families. Aggression from relatives hurts all the more the closer they are to us. Even abuse or murder stem from this blind love that can sometimes turn into a blind, raging, archaic energy.

Secondary feelings are substitutes for action. They come round again and again and make others feel angry and helpless. They do not move and so prevent resolution. An example is a young adult who cannot let go of anger towards a parent and misses the opportunity for separation, perhaps even into old age.

Foreign feelings are feelings that have been taken over from the family system. There is a conscience belonging to the family system that oversees the orders of relationships, and dictates that descendants unconsciously take on the feelings and inner state of relatives from a previous generation, even if they have never met these relatives or perhaps have never even heard of them. The condition which promotes this is that the previous relative was involved in some violation of the natural orders of the family system. This could be someone who was excluded from the family, or possibly someone who did not carry the consequences of his own actions. This particular dynamic is one of the sources of human tragedy. Driven by primary love, we unconsciously violate the natural orders and are required to pay the price. The Greek tragedies and those of Shakespeare are full of such examples (cf. Hellinger 2001).

Meta-feelings are feelings without emotion, for example, courage, serenity, or humility. They represent an acknowledgement of what is and make no judgements about good or evil. They are important for any leader of family constellations. Meta-aggression is the ability to lead someone to a place that is very difficult but demanded by the situation. The highest meta-feeling is wisdom, which allows one to distinguish what counts from what is not essential.

FOREIGN FEELINGS IN INDIVIDUAL WORK

In family constellations in an individual setting, it is important to remember that the feelings that develop in a client standing in the position of a different family member are usually secondary feelings or personal feelings. This means that when a client is acting as a representative of some relative, the process proceeds mostly on the biographical level, which often obscures the level of the natural orders of relationships. Thus, the feedback you get from the client more accurately reflects personal experiences. A woman, standing in her father's position, for example, will experience reactions that say more about her relationship with him and less about unconscious systemic entanglements. Nevertheless, it is usually therapeutically valuable for the client to be able to look through the eyes of another, and it can lead to resolution. Changing perspective, which has been adopted from gestalt therapy by NLP/NIG, clearly affirms this. It is not clear, however, that this will lead to the level of archaic systemic orders. Viewed systemically, there may be other, more relevant aspects that do not focus on the conscious memories of the client. A therapist with experience and good intuition, however, may be able to identify someone in the family who points to the client's entanglements. By changing positions or bringing in particular sentences and gestures, a systemically relevant solution may be found.

In speaking sentences of resolution, or "giving back the stone" (cf. p. 55), strong feelings may actually appear that lead to resolution. The effects confirm whether the client has reached the primary love that lies at the foundation of all family relationships.

Generally speaking, the presence of emotions is a sign that the client has been touched and a healing process set in motion, but it is not necessary. For some people, this process occurs with no externally visible signs.

Positive Intentions and Primary Love

There is a certain parallel between the "positive intention", which in the view of NLP belongs to every inner part, no matter how destructive and black, and the role played by primary love in family constellations. Like the members of a family, the parts of the self are members of an "inner family", and are also interested in the survival of the whole. An early belief, however, that may have been life-saving at an earlier time, has a limiting effect later or may even be life-threatening. Similarly, a child's urge to sacrifice himself for his parents' sake comes from the "positive intention" of primary love, whose goal, first and foremost, is that all family members grow up and live together. At the same time, it is exactly this influential drive of feelings that also entangles, preventing a child from having a full life, or even causing an early death.

Entanglements

An entanglement is an unconscious violation of the natural orders of relationship, driven by primary love. The family conscience will not allow members of the family system to be excluded, nor will it tolerate a member not carrying the full consequences of his or her own guilt. The effect of such breaches of conscience is that a later family member atones for the violation.

On the other hand, this unconscious atonement is also a violation of the natural orders in that the later family member is getting involved in the affairs of another, and in the process, doing damage to himself, but still not helping the original family member (cf. p. 43).

Unconscious, Co-Conscious, and the Greater Soul

C. G. Jung used the term "collective unconscious" to describe the realm of archetypal images that connect us all at a very deep level. In terms of actual interactive effects, we are always a part of our environment at an unconscious level, even when we feel ourselves to be isolated and fully separate. We could then speak of a co-conscious instead of an unconscious. In Bert Hellinger's work with family constellations, the term unconscious has become even broader. Rather than finding ourselves in the unconscious depths of our soul, we discover an innate archetypal family conscience controlling the basic natural orders of relationship (cf. next paragraph). This is what Hellinger calls "the greater soul". This concept makes it easier to understand the dynamics at work when unknown family members have effects on following generations. Such effects are inexplicable if we look only at the individual unconscious. The greater soul is a term appropriate to family constellation work, whereas the metaphor of the unconscious or co-conscious corresponds to those procedures drawn from NLP.

BASIC NATURAL ORDERS AND MOVEMENTS OF THE SOUL

From many years of experience with family constellations, Bert Hellinger discovered an archetypal, natural order of family relationships that appears to be innate. He has called these basic orders "the orders of love" (Hellinger, Weber a. Beaumont 2001). One aspect of these orders is based on a hierarchy in terms of time. Whoever was born first has a higher position (cf. p. 48).

In addition, no one who belongs to the family system can be excluded, and no one who comes later is allowed to meddle in the affairs of those who came before, even though primary love is often pushing for exactly that at an unconscious level. In family constellations where group members are used as representatives, we strive to find an order in which every member of the original family feel like they are in the right place. If we are successful in finding such an arrangement, and if the client can acknowledge this image of order, then he has discovered a significant life resource, one that allows the entanglements to dissolve. The primary task is always taking one's parents just as they are or were.

Recently, Bert Hellinger's work in groups has shifted, and the search for orders of love has dropped into the background and work with the movements of the soul has taken precedence. In this work, only the few most relevant persons are represented in a constellation, and they are instructed to follow their inner feelings, moving themselves until a direction towards resolution becomes clear. In such a resolution, designations of good and evil become meaningless. The client is sometimes part of the process from the beginning, but in other cases watches the whole thing from an outside position. In a certain sense, this search for the movements of the soul towards resolution is more appropriate for the tools of NIG than a search for an image of resolution. You only work up to the point where it becomes clear that a process has been initiated in the client. Then, you trust that a resolution will develop when the time is right (Hellinger 2002a).

EMPATHY AND REPRESENTATIVES' AWARENESS

It is undeniably true that we have the potential for empathic feelings. In many approaches to therapy, empathy is regarded as a primary prerequisite for therapeutic activity. It is also worth considering Steve de Shazer's comment that "there is no such thing as understanding, only more or less useful misunderstandings" (spoken comment). Even in the most highly developed empathic sensitivities, there is a component of projection and unconscious tendencies towards trying to influence others.

The research of Norbert Bischof and Doris Köhler-Bischof shows that by the age of three or four, a child has developed a "theory of mind". That means that we are capable of imagining ourselves in another person's shoes, even while remaining cognizant of the difference between our own viewpoint and that of the other (Bischof 2000). Children, in their critical dependence on others, have sensitive antennae for the feeling states of those around them. Up to a certain age they feel responsible for these states. We might assume that a part of the dynamics we have observed in family constellations, in which a child takes over someone else's guilt, can be traced back to this function.

Another experience that has only been made possible through family constellations is that of the representatives' awareness (Sparrer 2004). This means that in a constellation, people who are not part of the family system and are mostly neutral can develop feelings that match up with the person they are representing. There are various explanations for this phenomenon, but none to date have proved satisfactory. We can go back to the term "collective unconscious" (C. G. Jung) and assume an archetypal, innate order of relationships that could provide a neutral person with an awareness of any violations of these orders. This does not, however, fully explain the experience.

Constellations, Representations, and Imagining

We consider it important for a therapist or helping person to make clear whether the work is being done on the "biographical" level or on the level of archaic orders of relationships (cf. p. 28). Individual work with family images and family constellations, whether represented through symbols or sketches placed in position in the room, or imagined pictures, is different from work with representatives. The ability to look through the eyes of another is coloured by personal entanglements when it concerns one's own family, and therefore often makes a less powerful statement than is the case when the representative is not related to the system. We are of the opinion that clients should be informed of this and offered participation in a constellation group if appropriate. In many cases, the therapist's experience and intuition can provide a balancing factor.

On the other hand, there are certain advantages to the client standing in various positions, for example that of a parent, rather than observing a constellation of representatives from the outside. Clients who have done both report that their experience of repeating the family constellation using the NIG exercise of re-imprinting was an important complement to doing a constellation with representatives in a group. Resolution is also possible in a constellation done purely in the imagination (Franke 2002).

Nevertheless, we should consider a family constellation in an individual setting using spatial anchors, figures, or imagination, to be primarily in the realm of a "created reality". The medium of the representatives" awareness is missing. Accompanied by an experienced or very intuitive person, the process can still develop to reveal the underlying level of archaic orders of relationship illuminating the "created reality".

Paradoxical Structures of the Soul

"Things are always the opposite of how they are presented" said Bert Hellinger in speaking of relationships. It is actually often the

47

case that, for example, the person who appears to be the weakest turns out to have the most power in the system, or the perpetrators are revealed as victims, or the seemingly good are really the bad. It is not only on the physical level, but also on the psychological level of our existence that the other side of light is shadow, which has an equal effect. Occasionally, we feel shaken at the edge of our very existence when this side emerges in ourselves or in others. Every mother who has recognized that her well-meant, caring behaviour has, indeed, done serious harm to her child, is familiar with this experience.

Life Gestalting

The term *"Lebensgestaltung"*, shaping and creating one's own life, refers to the systemic-constructivist viewpoint that assumes that we are not merely subject to a given, unchangeable reality, but rather that we construct it ourselves through our fantasies of what is, or at least we participate significantly in the construction. We are not autonomous in our view of the world; we are dependent on our physiological make-up, our forefathers, and our environment, the way that others near and dear to us, particularly our mothers and fathers, see and experience the world. The constructivist view also has limits, particularly in physical givens, which we cannot change, but also in certain moulding factors from our family and culture that cannot be discarded.

In spite of the limitations, there seems to be some room for shaping our lives at the "biographical" level. This mainly comes up when we are able to look at a particular situation in a new light and learn to deal with our images in a better way. Strangely enough, the external circumstances sometimes then change as well. Family constellations, however, function at the level of the unchangeable orders of relationship, where there is no opportunity to shape anything differently, but only to acknowledge things the way they are. In NIG we utilize both of these aspects.

Time

Time plays an important role in both systemic-constructivist thinking and in systemic-phenomenological thinking. It is a part of our reality and problems often arise from attempts to avoid that fact.

In NIG, the life path confronts us with the reality of our own mortality, principally when life goals or the "old person in the future" is looked at.

In family constellations, time has particular meaning in the hierarchy of the system. "It seems that things gain a particular quality over time. What has lasted longer has priority over what has been in existence for a shorter time. What came earlier gains a quality of fullness over time." (Hellinger 2001).

In relation to families, this means that the injustices suffered or committed by earlier family members will be carried unconsciously by family members who come later. Those who have come before have priority over those who have been born later, who are required to pay the price for their ancestors (Hellinger 1996).

These are ideas that go against our "*Zeitgeist*" and against any sense of fairness and justice. They are, however, to be found in the tragedies of Shakespeare and the ancient Greeks, and they point to the archaic orders of relationship seen in family constellations.

4. Tools of Neuro-Imaginative Gestalting

Spatial Anchors

Anchors are stimuli for the senses that are connected to physiological or psychological reactions. Pavlov's famous dog, having repeatedly been given a piece of meat shortly after the sound of a bell, began to salivate at the sound of the bell even though he got no meat. Some people go into a state of panic at the sound of a siren because they had terrible experiences in night bombings during the war. We all know the everyday experience of melodies or smells triggering particular feelings or memories.

In NLP, anchors are mostly created with touch, whereas Robert Dilts developed spatial anchors and used places marked on the floor to represent particular images. The client was asked, for example, to assign a place on the floor to the inner image of the problematic present, to a future solution, and to a resource from the past. Pieces of paper were used to identify the images. By moving back and forth between the designated places, integration occurred. From a meta-position, that is, a neutral spot outside the marked area, it is possible to gain an overview of the whole and physically, mentally, and psychologically move in and out, disassociate and associate, as called for in the process.

The result is a psycho-geography in which you can not only mentally, but also physically move around in order to connect images, mix, or draw one aspect into the foreground, as is common in systemic therapy procedures.

In NIG, instead of blank papers or selected symbols, we use the previously described spontaneous sketches.

Looking Through the Eyes of Another

This underlying metaphor of NIG is one of the essential messages of a systemic approach. If we were able to consciously look through the eyes of another more often, and if we could make that a habit of our everyday lives, many things would be different. As one of the most important tools of NIG, this capability is described in detail.

Looking Through the Eyes of Another Family Member

In the NIG elements of the life path and the family image, for example, it was described how the image of the goal, the problematic present, and the resources from the past can be brought into awareness through the eyes of other family members, thereby providing new viewpoints. Besides broadening the view, this serves as a context orientation by relating to the family structure, which touches on the level of the natural orders of relationships.

Looking Through the Eyes of "The Old Person"

The "old person" (Büntig 1995) is an inner part of the self that can be introduced using various therapeutic elements. This person represents oneself shortly before the end of life, and is brought into the life path or re-imprinting exercises, providing the process with a special quality. Looking back from the end makes clear, among other things, that our life span is limited and the remaining time precious.

Looking Through the Eyes of the Child

Looking through the eyes of the child that one once was identifies the beginning of the life path. It brings the client into contact with a side that may still be lively in old age, or at least can become alive again: One's creativity and joy in living, and curiosity.

Looking Through the Eyes of a Resource Person

In the work with the life path and in re-imprinting, we are primarily concerned with finding the next step out of a problematic situation towards a solution. A resource person is someone who would most likely trust the client to be able to do this. For example, an aunt who always said, "N will manage". It is clear that looking through her eyes may give the client self-confidence, in addition to a new point of view.

Observing from the Meta-Position

The so-called meta-position is an element from NLP work with spatial anchors. It is a position that lies outside the particular inter-connections of persons or inner parts of the self (cf. p. 66). Standing in this position, we can look at our own situation or problematic relationships in a disassociated way, from a distance that allows a certain degree of neutrality. In the course of the procedure, returning to this place always makes it possible to look at the whole, calm down, and distinguish between what is essential and what is not. It is a process that is also appropriate for problem solving in everyday life, and implies a wisdom about life.

LIVING METAPHORS

The formulation "living metaphors" means that body position, posture, or activity work as "felt images" and are, therefore, messages to the unconscious (cf. p. 37).

In this regard, concretely "entering into the images", in which a person moves to and among images, is a living metaphor for complete and unified understanding – learning with mind and body.

Standing is a living metaphor for independence; moving is a living metaphor for change. The living metaphor of the "put yourself at the goal" has a different effect from a merely imagined goal or state of resolution. You find yourself physically in the state of having reached the goal (Sparrer 2004), and from that standpoint there is a different view looking backwards at the "next step to be taken" (cf. p. 76).

Bowing down, which plays a large role in family constellations, is a living metaphor for an attitude of respect for another.

CIRCULAR QUESTIONING

Circular questioning was originally developed by the Milan Team of Mara Selvini Palazzoli. During a family therapy, one of those present would be asked his opinion about the relationship between two other family members. For example, you might ask a child about her view of the relationship between another child in the family and the mother, or the father, and vice versa. This questioning technique was developed to an art by some therapists and was adapted and adopted in other systemic therapy approaches. Gunther Schmidt teaches an application for individual therapy that he has developed. The question might be, for example, "If your mother were here and I were to ask her how she sees your problem and what she would suggest as a solution, what would she say?" In this way, the client is encouraged to look through the eyes of that person at the supposed or actual causes, and to find various paths to a solution that are embedded in the context of the relationship.

This procedure can be used in a number of ways to support the context orientation of the various NIG elements.

RITUALS

Rituals are generally fixed procedures, and can therefore be repeated to achieve a psychological and sometimes also physical effect. We can look at them as messages to the unconscious.

In the current therapeutic scene it has become common to pay more attention to rituals. This is an understandable movement because healing rituals have played an important role in every culture. We can look at the therapeutic elements of NLP and NIG or family constellations as mini-rituals.

For example, the life path work is a ritual that can easily be repeated periodically. Family constellations in an individual setting also have the character of a ritual in a certain sense, although in this case a repetition may be either useless or possibly damaging, as it may disturb the unconscious process of a movement towards resolution.

Giving Back a Stone or Other Object

One of the mini rituals of family constellations that is used in NIG is giving back some object chosen to represent symbolically all that which has been taken over (a stone, a rucksack, or something else). The ritual is often accompanied by strong emotions and may have an immediate freeing effect. In any case, it can only be used when the client is in touch with his primary love for the parent in question, or becomes so. The therapist should pay particular attention to the client's unconscious body signals when he hands the object to the imagined mother or father. The client stands facing the parent and says: "I have tried to carry this for you, but it is too difficult for me. I am only the child. It belongs to you and it belongs to your dignity. I give it back to you in love." If there is too much aggression present, you can suggest the sentence: "I need a bit more time before I can give it back to you in love."

Bowing Down

Another ritual that occurs often in family constellations is bowing down before one's father or mother, or to a family member who perhaps died young. It does not symbolize subjugation or an indiscriminate bowing to authority, but rather signifies an acknowledgement of the fact that this family member was present earlier and therefore, according to the orders of relationship based on time, they have priority (cf. p. 48). Although as westerners we generally have very little experience with this kind of ritual behaviour, I am always astounded at the way that participants in constellations respond to it. You get the impression that there is an inner need for this kind of ritual.

A colleague who was very involved in constellation work once told me that she kept photos of her parents in her meditation corner so she could bow down to them every morning. "And every morning I experience something new," she added with a smile. She then reported, "A while ago I told my grown-up sons about this and they found the idea rather strange. A while later, one of them invited me to the opera, an idea that would never have entered his mind earlier. Then the other one suddenly suggested going on a holiday with me for a few days. You can imagine how happy that made me!"

The Line of Mothers or Fathers

(This ritual is described on p. 123).

Rituals in the Imagination

There is a short ritual that I usually recommend to mothers who are worried about a child. "Whenever you feel overwhelmed with your

54

worries, or every day at a specific time, remember a situation in which this child looked at you with gratitude. As you do this, think of a colour that you feel would be a good one for your child and mentally send it out to him or her." These instructions are used as an introduction before proceeding with a resource orientation in the imagination. Even though it probably does not change anything in the current situation for the child, it does help to keep the parent from burdening the child further with exaggerated worries.

Many ideas and techniques for conducting constellations in the imagination can be found in the book *In My Mind's Eye*, by Ursula Franke (2003).

Spoken Sentences

Beliefs

NLP experience has shown that traumatic experiences in one's youth lead to certain beliefs that are held throughout life, even when the external circumstances have long since changed. For example, a child who was laughed at or scolded when she revealed her feelings will adopt the belief that she dare not show feelings and will carry this belief into adulthood, thereby limiting and possibly harming herself. Changing such a negative belief is an important therapeutic concern in this approach.

In re-imprinting, (cf. p. 97), it is useful to ask about the beliefs of the child from back then, or using the element of "two sides" (cf. p. 106), one can ask the client to stand in each position, formulating sentences expressing the beliefs of each side. It should be noted whether the sentence, seen in regard to the current situation, has changed, and if a positive belief can be drawn from the process. In the above- mentioned case the sentence might be, "With certain people I can certainly show my feelings."

Sentences of Resolution or Sentences of Power

The sentences that resolve entanglements in family constellations, which Bert Hellinger has called "Sentences of Power", are an important part of NIG (e. g. Hellinger 2002b). In our opinion, it is necessary to have some experience with family constellations in order to work effectively with these. With an adequate understanding gained from the literature, one can certainly suggest a sentence of resolution for a client if it seems to suit the situation. It will be clear whether it "fits" or not.

THE ATTITUDE OF THE THERAPIST

Bert Hellinger has determined that a constellation leader should be without intention, courageous, and in harmony with reality (cf. "meta-feelings" p. 43). He must refrain from helping one person at the cost of the whole system. The leader's attention remains concentrated on the whole. A related skill is being able to reduce what is said to the essential minimum, which means the facts and events that affect the whole family, and the ability to recognize which persons are relevant.

In NLP, the aim is to adjust the inner map of what "used to be" to match the present situation. The therapist or helper looks primarily at the "personal reality", that is, the biography of the client. Rather than "acknowledging what is", the focus is on opportunities for change.

In NIG, depending on which therapeutic element is being used, we move back and forth between these two approaches. This corresponds to the reality of the soul as described in "The existential Paradox" (cf. p. 183).

In both methods, the therapist is basically an assistant who chooses the appropriate tool for the situation and passes it on to the client.

Observing and Seeing

Careful observation of a client's unconscious body signals is the basis of systemic therapy. Observing in this way, the therapist is focussed and keenly aware of any changes in facial expression, breathing, or position of the body.

Particularly for family constellations in groups, but also in individual work, the therapist must be trained to see the whole. This is an inner attitude as well as a skill that can be learned. A help is to look, in relaxed concentration, at the whole picture through a soft focus lens – rather like looking out of the corner of your eye.

Using the Non-Dominant Hand

Writing or sketching with the non-dominant hand allows the unconscious part of the representation to have a voice. The unpracticed hand (for right-handed people, the left hand, and for left-handed people, the right hand) is less under conscious control and closer to the unconscious. Interestingly enough, in using the non-dominant hand, you actually write and draw like a child. It also reassures clients because it disposes of any demand for perfection.

If this method is too difficult for a client, or if the therapist has forgotten to give the proper instructions at the beginning of the procedure, a resulting dominant-hand sketch can still be used. The non-dominant hand merely increases the power of a statement, generally speaking.

5. Practical Guide to NIG

PROCEDURES

This chapter presents general practical information about working with NIG, followed by a detailed description of each of the so-called NIG exercises or NIG elements (cf. p. 64). Regardless of which of the NIG elements you choose, all the exercises are based on the same procedures. As we have already mentioned, sketches are drawn spontaneously using the non-dominant hand and positioned on the floor in the space available. As the client lays out the sketches, he is aware of not only the visual aspect, but also experiences the images physically. In this holistic way, the quality and strength of expression in a single drawing becomes clear, as well as the relationship between the sketches in various positions. This awareness is heightened and expanded through the addition of a blank sheet of paper for the meta-position, and through movements back and forth between the papers.

MATERIAL

Although a spontaneous sketch can be drawn with any ballpoint pen, a choice of various pencils and chalks encourages a creative process. In practice, we have found that oil pastel chalks are available in a wide range of colours and allow for blocks of colour as well as contour lines. Alternatively, or in addition, felt pens, crayons, or coloured pencils may be offered.

A practical and affordable choice of paper is white typing paper (A4). This is a size that allows a person to stand on it and it is relatively resistant to tearing.

58

If there is no desk or table available, the cardboard backing from a pad of drawing paper serves well as a support for drawing the sketches.

It is naturally advantageous if there is enough space to lay out the sketches, preferably on a floor with a relatively smooth surface. If this is not the case, improvisation can overcome many obstacles in the space. For example, if a client is of the opinion that the desirable place for a paper is much further out than the space allows, the client can simply imagine the perfect distance and that usually suffices.

Variations and Adaptations

In addition to the sketches described above, there are other materials and techniques that can be used for the NIG exercises described in the next chapter. Although sketches drawn by the client's own hand are undeniably valuable, they are not appropriate in every situation, for example, organizational consulting or coaching. Time factors may dictate the use of other materials since drawing sketches takes time that may not always be available. Additionally, an individual client's preferences need to be considered.

A practical alternative to sketches is the use of coloured pieces of felt, the size of a piece of typing paper. These are available in hobby shops in every colour, and are relatively inexpensive. They are a pleasure to work with as the client can choose the colours according to the emotional tone of the representation. One can, of course, also use coloured paper or pieces of cloth.

When the therapist or helper chooses not to use sketches or felt pieces, for example in consulting and coaching in companies or institutions, symbols or forms suitable to the situation can be used.

As already mentioned, two important parts of NIG are the family image and family constellations. The family members can be represented in sketches or by symbols cut from felt: red circles for females and blue rectangles for males, each with a cut-out on one side to indicate direction.

Figure: Circle and rectangle with cut-outs

People can also be represented by coloured felt pieces (A4 size), coloured paper, or pieces of cloth, each with a cut out to indicate direction.

Last but not least, we should also point out that one can use group participants instead of spatial anchors. In the case study on p. 159, you will find a practical example of work with the NIG element of "two sides" which developed into a constellation with group participants representing the inner parts of the person.

Interview Questions

For an initial interview in the NIG approach, a modified form of de Shazer's technique (de Shazer 1988) works very well. When the client has explained what the issue is, the therapist asks the question, "What is your image of a resolution in the future, a state in which you no longer need help?" This type of question acts as a message to the unconscious. The spotlight is shifted from the very beginning away from the realm of the problem into the realm of solutions. (Gunther Schmidt). When the time seems right, the next question is to ask about when and where things are better. This question has the function of allowing the realm of the solution to become clearer.

Based on his experience that mobilizing resources is the basis of successful brief therapy, de Shazer pays attention only to times when things have been better, or times in the course of a day when things are better. In addition, he asks about what the effects would be if by some miracle the problem was unexpectedly resolved: "How would you notice it? What would you do, then?" In this way, the client's unconscious is focused on an image of resolution. In NIG, the client can immediately draw a sketch of the answer that is then put aside for use later in an NIG exercise.

An interview for a family constellation is different. In this case, you ask about events that have affected the whole family, such as early deaths, exile, Nazi entanglements, serious illnesses, crimes committed by individual family members, inheritance quarrels, and other such events. The interview is kept brief with the question: "What has happened in your family?" Too many details detract from what is essential (cf. Hellinger 2002a).

60

Sketches

As mentioned, in NIG you can include sketching the problems, imagined resolutions, etc. in the initial interview, even if you have no idea how you may work with them later. This opens up a different level of communication, which often moves organically into the therapeutic process. In my experience, when the client has done a few sketches, one can immediately ask him to lay out the drawings according to an inner picture. This may be before the therapist is clear about which NIG element may develop. In doing this, you discover how the individual elements partially overlap and complement one another.

In looking together at sketches, particularly those drawn with the non-dominant hand, the therapist and the client will notice particulars that can be seen as signals or messages from the unconscious. For example, the choice of colour, lines, and the spatial relationships of elements on the paper, among other things, will sometimes communicate something that was previously unconscious or difficult to express in words.

Whereas children are usually happy to be asked to draw a sketch, young people and adults may object if they consider themselves to be artistically lacking in talent or skill. In such cases, the therapist explains that it does not have to do with artistic expression, but rather to help the client later identify the problem and the solution on paper. Besides, most people drawing with the non-dominant hand (right-handed people draw with the left hand) do not produce a "beautiful" picture in the usual sense of the word. The therapist will also point out that any size and any kind of representation is acceptable: symbols such as circles, rectangles, numbers, or letters; one colour or colourful abstract sketches; realistic representations.

If the client still feels reluctant to sketch despite the explanation, shift to one of the other materials as described above.

Working with the Sketches

In the various NIG exercises, the therapist asks the client for sketches not only of the problem and the state of resolution, but also, for example, for representations of people, capabilities, or positive steps taken in the past. Regardless of what the sketch is about, the client describes the completed sketch in his own words. For the client himself, it is the first step towards verbalizing his pictured statement. For the therapist, it makes clear what the client is trying to express. The therapist is focused on understanding during this process and so can ask questions for clarification, but makes no comments or judgements (cf. p. 24).

When the client has found a satisfactory place on the floor for the sketches, he stands on the papers, moving back and forth between them, and notices his reactions in various places. The client's attention should be primarily on body reactions, including changes in breathing, facial expressions, muscle tension, emotional reactions, and movements. Eye movements and the direction the person is facing play an important role. The body serves as a reliable barometer for capturing essentials, and prevents "head" interpretations and speculations about a relationship or the facts of the matter. Sometimes physical reactions are so minimal that the client is not even aware of them, for example, the suggestion of an upper-body movement backwards, a slight swaying, holding his breath, barely perceptible movements of a finger, or a slight raising of his shoulders. In such cases it is helpful for the therapist to draw the client's attention to these reactions, or to ask him to intensify the movement in order to make the emotional message more accessible.

TIME FRAMES

Every therapist has her own time rhythm, according to which the length of a session is arranged. The NIG exercises can be fit into this time frame. Sessions of 60 to 90 minutes have proven satisfactory. If an exercise has not been completed within the time allotted, the work can be ended at an appropriate place and the client is asked to stand on the sketches from time to time or to add new sketches on his own. If the interrupted exercise is taken up again in the next session, it is often amazing to see what changes have occurred in the client's viewpoint during the intervening time. An initial move in the direction of a solution frequently has a stronger effect than a completely worked-out strategy for a solution.

The intervals between sessions are arranged according to the issue involved, the client's wishes, and the therapist's setting and methods. Generally speaking, it is usual in solution-orientated systemic brief therapy to conduct sessions with longer intervals between them in order to leave enough room for the client's self-organization.

DEALING WITH STRONG EMOTIONS

If strong emotions are touched off, for example, through contact with traumatic childhood memories, remember that the meta-position or the neutral observer always makes it possible to dissociate from one's own personal situation, that is, to be aware of it separate from oneself. This change of perspective can bring about an astounding change in the client's way of experiencing even strong emotions such as fear or rage, which may have previously felt uncontrollable,.

If a client is extremely entangled in emotions (cf. p. 41) when standing in a particular position, it is possible and sometimes very helpful to move to the position of the neutral observer. From this position, the structure of the sketches can be taken in safely, and the position of individual papers changed. Suggestions may be offered and some insight can be gained. It is always surprising to see the clarity that develops in this position and the power of self-organization in motion from this place.

6. Description of Procedures

How to Use the Descriptions of Procedures

Overview

The following procedures for the various exercises or elements of Neuro-Imaginative Gestalting (NIG) are a guide to the first practical steps using this method. The step-by-step procedures described here are not recipes to be followed exactly, but merely basic structures. With increasing experience you will gain more freedom in using them. To begin with, if you feel unsure about the procedures, make a photocopy of the description to have on hand during a session and refer to it whenever the need arises.

The sequence of the elements is constructed so that the reader / user moves from the simple to the more complex. For example, the first exercise, "the meta-position", lends itself well to getting to know the basic principle of a "view from the outside" in an uncomplicated way.

The next element, the "interruption of patterns", follows naturally from the work with the "meta-position". In this exercise, besides looking at the problem, we also look at exceptions to the problem. In the extended form, "positive intentions" enter into the picture.

The element "developing skills" leads to work with resources, which plays a central role in the following "life path". In the extended version of the "life path", there is increasing differentiation in the inclusion of resources.

The two elements "family image" and "family constellations" form the heart of NIG, since the previous procedures are now expanded to include the family. In "presenting the family image" we use "looking through the eyes" of individual family members to gain new and different points of view. Various possibilities for integrating

Hellinger's family constellation work with NIG are included for therapists who have experience with family constellations.

In the element "re-imprinting", we look for the causes of a problem by going back on a time-line. There is a description of how to integrate family constellations with this exercise.

Working with ambivalence is presented in the element called "two sides". In its basic form, this exercise is concerned with a dialogue between two contrasting sides and the "positive intentions" of each. In the extended form, common features between the "positive intentions" of both sides lead to solutions. The description of the NIG elements is rounded off with a collection of possible homework assignments.

The description of procedures is written as instructions from the therapist to the client, or in the case of self-helpers, for proceeding alone. In addition to the step-by-step descriptions of exercises, graphics have been included for clarity. These graphics portray only the most important steps of the procedures and serve as a reminder of what comes next.

Structures: A Basis for Creative Processes

For first attempts at using NIG, it is advisable to begin with the simpler exercises and gradually gain experience with the procedures and their effects. With more familiarity, the practitioner can choose a particular exercise based on the way a session has developed. We have found it useful to begin with two sketches, for example, the problem in the present and the resolution in the future, and then see which direction things take from there.

The description of the NIG elements is detailed and complete in order to facilitate a start in the work. The actual course of an exercise, however, is largely dependent on the issue at hand and the reactions of the client, as well as the personality and professional background of the therapist.

When a therapist or practitioner feels comfortable following the flow of the NIG exercises, he will soon notice that the work goes beyond the initial framework or is modified in some way. For example, it is not always necessary for someone to stand on each and every sketch or spatial anchor. It might be more useful to observe the process with a particular emphasis, such as through the eyes of the neutral observer or an important resource person.

The detailed procedural structures are meant to be a basis for creative use of the NIG elements. From this basis, therapists and practitioners will develop their own procedures and combine the NIG elements with other ways of working.

THE META-POSITION

The View from Outside

As mentioned, a meta-position is one of the basic figures in the therapeutic procedures that has been drawn from NLP (cf. p. 52). If you are working with spatial anchors, as is normally the case in NIG, you have the client sketch her problem and lay it on the floor. Then you ask her to position a blank sheet in such a way that she can look at her problem from a distance as a neutral observer, as if she were another person. This is not a case of "looking through the eyes of another", but of looking at oneself *as if one were another person* (cf. p. 51). This perception is called dissociation.

If the client stands in the problem position, it is experienced from an inner perspective, including body awareness. This experience is called associative or self-representative awareness.

The view from the meta-position often results in amazing changes in a client's way of seeing things. Through a change of perspective from the inner view to the outer perspective, perhaps repeatedly, negative feelings that had previously been regarded as insurmountable may diminish. Beliefs that had had a limiting function may be recognized as strengthening resources. In many cases, a movement to the meta-position is sufficient to deal with the issue at hand. In other cases it may prompt the next therapeutic step.

In the case of self-help, putting differences to work "(de Shazer), that is, the movement back and forth between the associative and dissociative positions, can be very helpful in gaining a new perspective on one's own situation. The meta-position can also be incorporated into group exercises in many different ways.

Depending on the issue and personal preferences, the meta-position has various names. For some people it is a "neutral observer" or a "neutral advisor". Others are more comfortable with the "wise woman" or the "wise old man".

In any case, the therapist should make certain that the meta-position is far enough from the configuration of sketches to allow a view from outside. It is also important for the client to verbally acknowledge that she is looking at herself through another's eyes. As a neutral observer, she might say something like, "I would advise Ms. Jones to put her own needs in the foreground." Or as the wise woman she might say, "From my point of view, Jane already knows what the solution is. She just needs to trust her own inner voice."

Description of Procedure: Meta-Position

1. What is your problem and what do you want?
2. Sketch an image of the current problem, using your non-dominant hand, and lay it in an appropriate place on the floor.
3. Use a blank piece of paper to mark the meta-position (neutral observer, or other) and lay it at some distance from the problem sketch.

4. Stand on the problem sketch and pay attention to your physical and emotional reactions. How are you standing? How are you breathing? How are you feeling? What do you notice?
5. Stand in the meta-position. What is different in this position? What is the same? How does the neutral observer see the problem from here?
6. Return to the problem in the present. Notice your posture, your breathing, your feelings, your position. How do you experience the problem now? What has changed, and what has remained the same?
7. Go back to the meta-position again and notice the differences. What would you advise that person with that problem? Have you got any suggestions, ideas, or recommendations for this person?

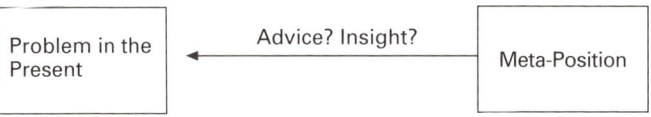

8. If the exercise has achieved what you wanted, end it here. If you need more clarification, repeat the back and forth movement between the problem and the meta-position, or continue on to the next exercise, "interrupting patterns".

INTERRUPTING PATTERNS

Behaviour Patterns: Problems and Exceptions

"Interrupting patterns" contains elements from NLP as well as elements drawn from the solution orientated brief therapy of de Shazer (cf. de Shazer 1988). De Shazer saw problems and also exceptions to the problems as behaviour patterns that produced a particular state of feeling. He described this work as an attempt to define the difference between the complaint and the exceptions to the complaint (de Shazer 1988). This means that we are primarily interested in discovering the patterns of behaviour that lead to the problem and those that lead to exceptions to the problem. By using the differences, instead of feeling like a victim subjected to seemingly arbitrary feelings, the client can see his own participation in how he feels. With the question, "When is it better?", the client becomes aware that in certain behaviour patterns, he moves along the path leading to the "exceptions to the problems", whereas a different behaviour cements the problem in place. The client is motivated to interrupt old behaviour patterns and turn his attention to behaviour that leads to exceptions.

The client makes a sketch for the current problem and a sketch of exceptions to this problem. ("How is it when things are better?") With the help of the neutral observer, he can distinguish the differences, the common features, and the positive intentions of both the problem pattern and the non-problem pattern. The neutral observer supports him in discovering the differences in behaviour in the two patterns and offers recommendations for certain behaviours.

In the "extended version of interrupting patterns", an additional change of perspective is brought in through circular questioning. The client is concerned with the point of view of those people who are important to him. He considers their opinions about potential behavioural changes and in doing so broadens his own range of vision.

Description of Procedure: Basic Structure of Interrupting Patterns

1. What is your problem and what do you want?
2. Make two sketches, using your non-dominant hand.
   - One picture of the current problem
   - One picture of exceptions to the problem ("How is it when things are better (good)?")
3. Lay the sketches on the floor somewhere in this space.
4. Choose a position outside the space (meta-position: neutral observer).

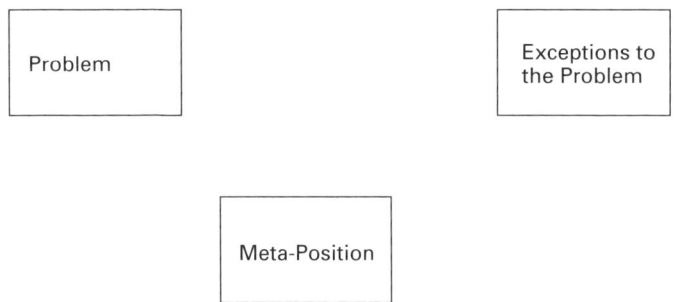

5. Stand on the problem sketch and pay attention to your physical and emotional reactions. How are you standing? How is your breathing? How are you feeling? What do you notice?
6. Move to the position of exceptions to the problem and do the same.
7. Change to the meta-position and look at the two sketches from the outside.
   - What differences do you notice?
   - What do you see that is the same?
   - What is the positive intention of each?

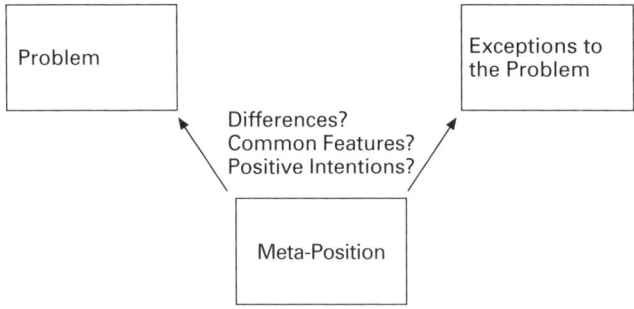

8. Return to the problem. What differences do you notice? What is the same and what has changed?
9. Go to the exceptions to the problems and do the same.
10. Go back to the meta-position.
    - What has changed?
    - What behaviour leads to problems and what leads to the exceptions?
    - What behaviour would you advise from this position?
    - Perhaps a completely different behaviour occurs to you?

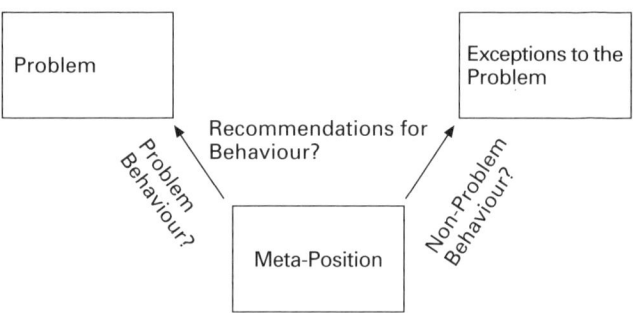

11. Return to the problem. How do you feel about the recommendations from the neutral observer? Do you agree or have you got objections or suggestions for improvement?
12. Go back to the position of exceptions to the problem and do the same.

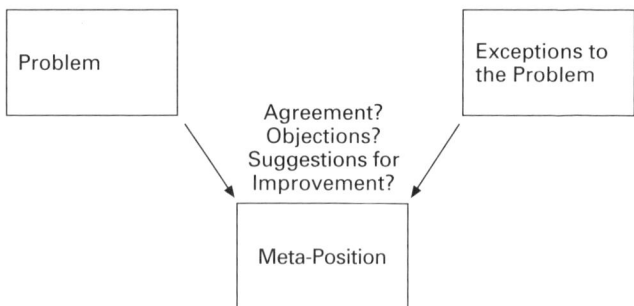

13. If there are objections to the recommendations for behaviour, you can continue with the "extended version of interrupting patterns" as described in the next section. If the alternative behaviour is satisfactory to both sides, you can end here.

It may be appropriate, however, to create a sketch of the relevant changes of behaviour and put it in the appropriate place on the floor.

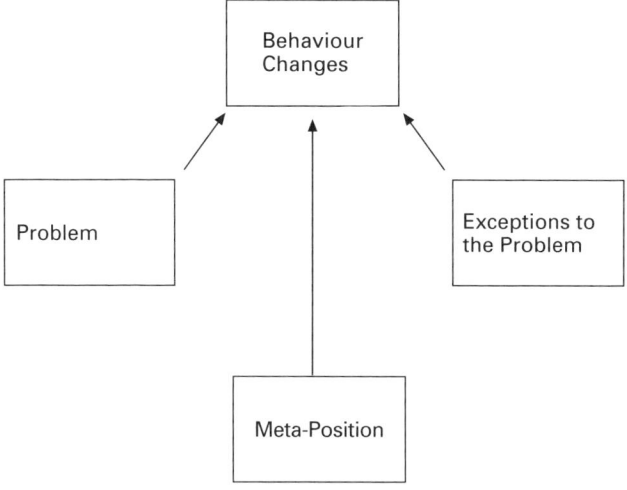

14. Stand in the position of the behaviour changes. Pay attention to your physical and emotional reactions.
15. Move first to the problem position and then to the exceptions to the problem. How do the behaviour changes look from each of these positions?
16. Close by standing in the meta-position and noticing your experience of the whole thing.

Description of Procedures: Interrupting Patterns – Extended Version
1. Follow points one to twelve of the basic structure of interrupting patterns.
2. If there are objections from the position of the problem or from the exceptions to the problem in response to the suggestions for behavioural changes, return to stand in the meta-position.
   – How do you experience the objections from this position?
   – What insights have you gained?
   – Have the recommendations for a change in behaviour al tered?

71

3. If so, stand in the position of the problem and the exceptions, one after another, and notice the changes.

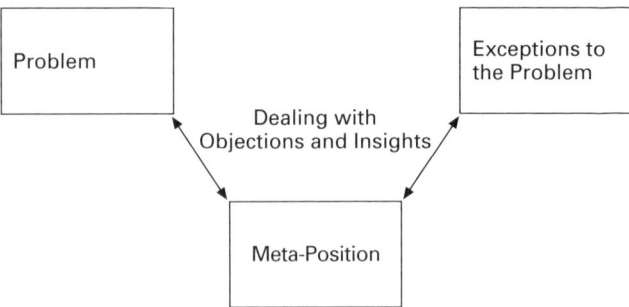

4. Step to the meta-position and think about a person who is important to you, someone within or outside of your family. Ask yourself the following questions:
   - How do you think this person sees the problem?
   - How do you think this person sees the exceptions to the problem, that is, when things are good?
   - How do you think this person sees the possible changes in behaviour?
   - How do you think this person sees the objections to a change in behaviour?
5. Draw a sketch of this person and find a good place for it on the floor. Stand in this position and notice the new point of view and information.

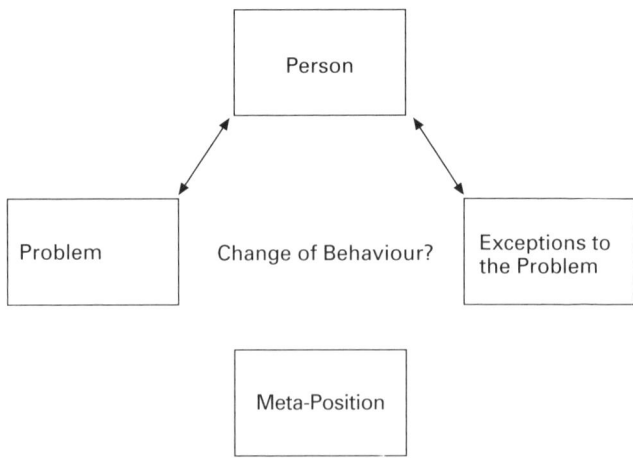

6. Stand first in the position of the problem and then in the position of the exceptions and notice any changes.
7. Close the exercise as in steps thirteen to sixteen described in the basic structure of interrupting patterns.

DEVELOPING SKILLS

Positive Experiences as Anchors

The NIG exercise "developing skills" illustrates an important procedure in systemic therapy. Instead of working with a "big" problem, we turn our attention to the mastery of a very simple skill. If the client has the experience of successfully learning a new skill, the initial problem may take on a different status, may become more qualified, or may resolve. The underlying concept is the circular reciprocal process in the human psyche. A positive experience in one area serves as an anchor and influences other areas as well (Dilts, Halbom a. Smith 1990). In any case, this procedure should address skills the client would like to possess. Skills and capabilities that the client used to have and would like to regain are also appropriate for this exercise. Even if there is no urgent problem, this exercise can be tossed in as a self-help tool for a more conscious shaping and creating of one's own life.

In this exercise, starting with the desired skills, attention is turned towards capabilities or actions that have already been mastered and that were helpful. These serve later, in the course of the exercise, as resources to support confidence that the new skill can also be learned. The position of the neutral observer accompanies this process by guiding new points of view and awareness.

Description of Procedures: Developing Skills
1. What skills or capabilities would you like to develop or perfect?
2. Find three skills or activities that you do well and that you feel good doing.
3. Imagine yourself in one of these activities. How do you move? What do you see, hear, feel, taste, and smell? With your non-dominant hand, draw a sketch of this activity.
4. Do the same with the other two activities.
5. Get in touch with the skill or activity that you would like to develop. Imagine yourself the way you are capable – or not

capable – of doing this. How do you move? What do you see, hear, feel, taste, and smell? Draw a sketch of this capability.

6. Lay all four sheets of paper on the floor. Choose exactly the relationships that you feel are right and let yourself be guided by your physical feeling.

7. Choose a place for a blank sheet of paper that is outside (meta-position, neutral observer). Stand in this position and check that each individual sketch is placed correctly. Are the spatial relationships between them right?

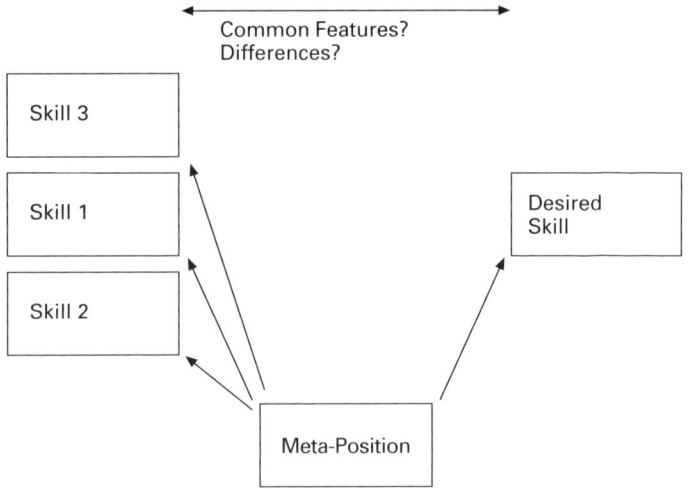

8. Stand in the position of skills one to three, one after another, and then move to the position of the desired skill. Pay attention to your physical and emotional reactions. How are you standing? How are you breathing? How do you feel? What do you notice? What do the skills have in common and what is different between them?

9. Move back to the meta-position and look at the whole picture again from the outside. Has anything changed for you? Can you see any new connections or any new qualities?

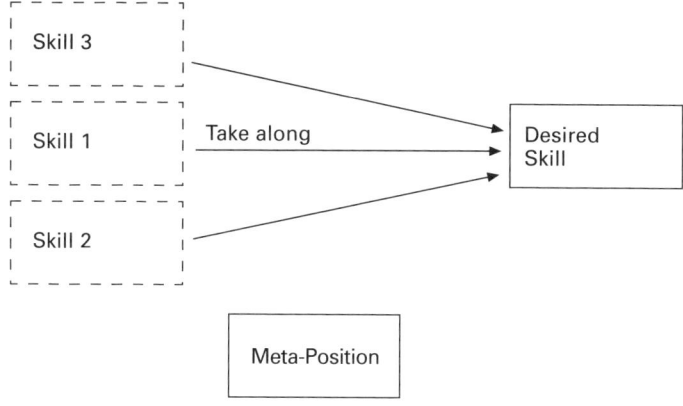

10. Go and collect skills one to three, standing on each one again briefly to notice your state in each place. Take the sketches with you to the position of the desired skill.
11. Stand in this position holding the other sketches in your hand. How do you feel now? How are you standing? How are you breathing? What do you notice? What is different from before and what has remained the same?
12. Lay out the skills one to three near the desired skill and go to stand in the meta-position. What has changed?

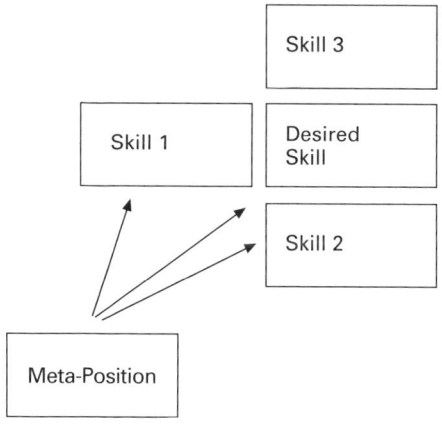

13. Collect the sketches of skills one to three again and put them under the desired skill. Stand on the whole stack. How do you feel now in this position? What does this tell you?

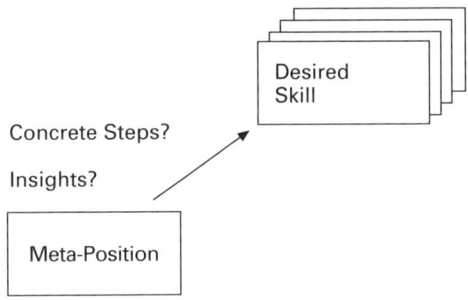

Concrete Steps?

Insights?

Meta-Position

14. Return to the meta-position. What insights do you have? What concrete steps could be taken to master the desired skill?

15. Carry the sketches of skills one to three with you for a while, particularly when you want to activate the desired skill.

THE LIFE PATH

The Life Path: Finding Resources for the Next Step

The life path is based on the time line of NLP. It provides a way of discovering resources or sources of strength needed for the appropriate next step out of a difficult situation towards an appropriate goal. Initially, the image of a goal is concerned with the immediate problem situation and with finding concrete steps that may possibly contribute to a resolution of this problem. It can, however, also be expanded to include life tasks and the very purpose of life. An appropriate goal is an important resource and a source of strength that supports the right steps towards the goal (cf. p. 32).

The Basic Structure

No matter how complex the configuration of the work on an individual life path, the starting point is always made up of three components:

- The present, with its problems
- The appropriate goal
- Resources from the past

These three components are represented on pieces of paper are laid out in the room. This creates time intervals within the space and allows for moving freely between the past, present, and future. This configuration changes the linear concept of time because it becomes clear that it is not only the past that has an effect on the present and the future, but also vice versa;, the concept of the future has an effect on our state in the present, and the present state influences the picture we have of the past. The systemic therapy view is of a "circular time" in which past, present, and future have reciprocal effects. This exercise allows us to physically experience that quality.

When in the Therapeutic Process?
The life path can, in principle, be woven into any phase of the therapeutic process. If it is brought in at the beginning of a series of individual sessions, the client will be introduced immediately to a way of working that is solution- and resource-orientated. For those who are accustomed to having all of their thoughts and feelings attached to their problems, this can mean an enormous change. Turning attention away from problems and possible causes and looking towards sources of strength and potential changes may be a great relief. The life path exercise can also be a support for overcoming health problems. When an appropriate health goal has been worked out, memories of healing processes in the past are incorporated as resources.

It is advisable to spend two to three sessions on the life path so that the client has time between sessions to work more intensively with possible goals and sources of strength from his life.

If other aspects are in the foreground at the beginning of the therapeutic work, the life path can be introduced at a later time to anchor the results of the therapy and work on making life changes. The end of a therapy sequence is also an appropriate time to look ahead with strength using the life path exercise. It is particularly interesting to repeat the life path work, perhaps weeks or years later. Sometimes it becomes clear that either the goal or the resources have changed in the meantime. The life path (and the repetition of the work) provides a way of facing new crises, particularly as a self-help tool.

The life path exercise in its basic form is also applicable as a group exercise, either at the beginning of a group or at the end of the time together (cf. p. 117).

Criteria for an Appropriate Goal

We all carry a concept, more or less consciously, of our life's path and our future. This inner image guides us in our actions and our feelings whether we know it and want it or not. An inappropriate image of the future can have serious consequences, whereas an appropriate concept of goals awakens physical and psychological energies. Therefore, working on the concept of a goal requires particular care (cf. p. 32 f.) When a client comes into therapy with a concrete problem, the image of a goal might be a situation in which the problem has been solved or been altered in such a way that the client can deal with it alone.

Criteria for an appropriate goal are:

1. Is your goal formulated positively (for example "I would like to give myself more free time" instead of "I want to work less")?
2. Are you yourself active in regards to this goal (for example, "I would like to change the way I act with my wife", instead of "I want my wife to behave differently.")?
3. How will you know when you have reached your goal?
4. Is this goal consistent with your current beliefs and experience?
5. Do you agree to the possible consequences for you and for others?

The last criterion is a departure from goal setting in NLP and takes into consideration that reaching a goal has consequences for others. Systemic thinking includes the idea that a good goal should also serve others, or at least not harm them. A good resolution is good for everybody.

Description of Procedures: Basic Structure: "Life Path"

1. What is the problem and what is your concept of the future? Is your goal appropriate according to the above criteria?
2. Sketch with your non-dominant hand:
   - An image of your current situation with its problem (problem in the present).

- An image of the state in the future in which this problem has been solved or is so altered that you can deal with it yourself (goal).
3. Inside yourself, go into your past. Remember concrete steps you have taken that had a positive effect and helped you to move forward on your way (for example, final exams, decision to get married, etc.). Make a sketch of each step on a separate piece of paper (resource 1, 2, 3, 4 …).
4. Lay out your life path on the floor, including all the sketches.

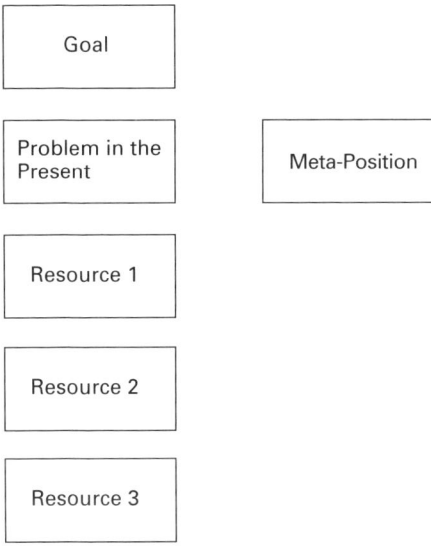

Note: This diagram presents the sketches in a time line from the past to the present to the future in a straight line. Actually, the time line can just as easily take a winding path. Even when a resource from the past is put in the future spatially, there is usually some inner logic to it.

5. Choose a position outside for the meta-position and mark it with a blank sheet of paper. Stand in this position and look at your life path from this perspective. Are the sketches in the right places? What do you notice?
6. Stand in the present problem position and pay attention to your physical and emotional reactions. How are you stand-

ing? How are you breathing? How are you feeling? What do you notice?

7. Move forwards to your goal concept and do the same thing. What changes do you notice?

8. Turn around and look back at the whole thing , particularly the "next step", from the present to the resolution, where you are now standing. Do you have any concrete ideas what this step might be?

9. Go back to the position of the present problem and see how it feels now. Move backwards into the past to resource 1. How do you feel here? Move to each additional resource and notice any changes.

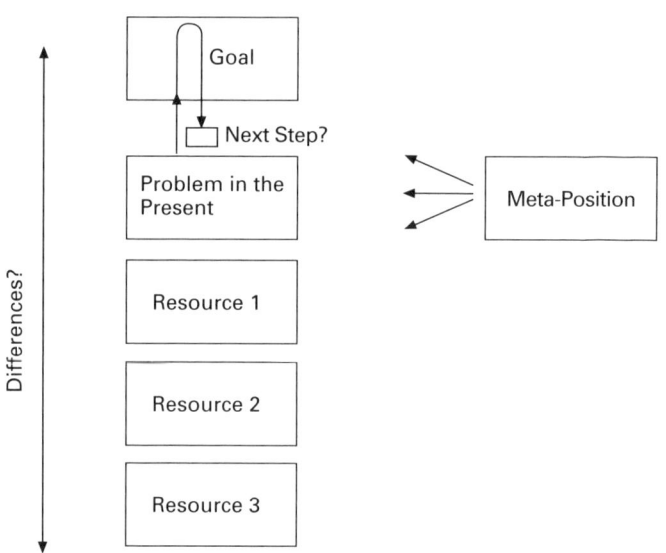

10. When you have reached the earliest resource, turn around and look at the future again. Look at the whole pattern at once from this perspective. What step does the little child see the adult making to come to a solution? Move slowly in the direction of the future (goal) and take your resources with you by collecting the papers as you move.

11. Stop at the image of the present and lay the resource sketches underneath this paper. What has changed? How do you feel now compared to how you felt in this position earlier? What

concrete steps can you see yourself taking to move towards your goal?

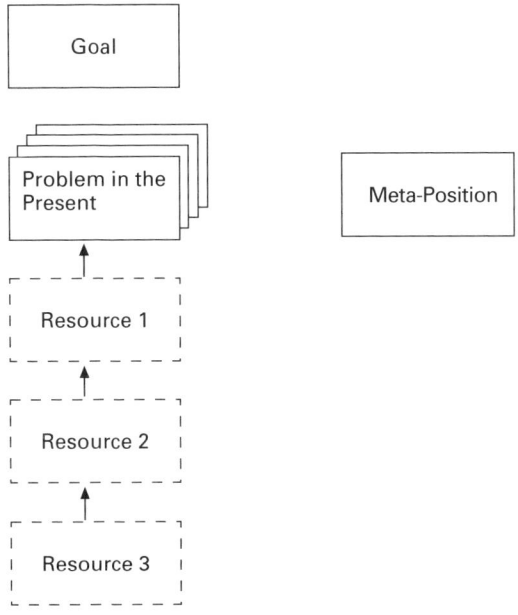

12. Return to the position in the future, taking your resources with you, and lay them underneath the sketch of the goal. Now look back at the present from the position of having reached your goal. What steps did you take and what resources helped you to do this?

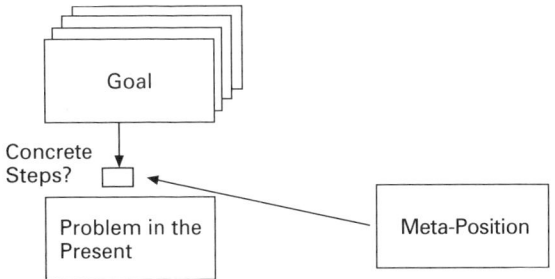

13. Stand in the meta-position and look at your life path from the outside. Has it changed for you? What concrete steps can you see yourself taking next?

14. Carry these sketches of strength with you in some form for a while.
15. Repeat the exercise, perhaps after a few months. What steps have you taken? How does your concept of a goal look now? What resources have been particularly useful? What new resources have appeared? Which "next steps" have emerged?

Description of Procedures: "Life Path" – Extended Version
Whereas the basic structure of the life path is appropriate for individual, group, or self-help use, the following extended version is meant more for use by professionally trained colleagues.

Included as resources in this version are: A resource person, other important people, places, animals, or plants. These support a context orientation that is less pronounced in the basic structure of the life path.

1. What is the problem and what is your concept of your goal? Make sure that the goal is consistent with the criteria for an appropriate goal.
2. Sketch with your non-dominant hand:
   - An image of your present situation with its problem (problem in the present).
   - An image of a state in the future in which this problem has been solved or is so altered that you can deal with it your self (goal).
3. Inside yourself, go into your past. Remember some important "next steps", decisions, or meaningful experiences that had positive effects and that helped you to move forward on your way. Make a sketch of these, each on a separate piece of paper.
4. Think about people who have helped you to take these steps. Make a separate sketch of each of these people.
5. Which of these people would be most likely to believe that you can overcome your current problem (resource person)?
6. Are there any memories of places, animals, or plants that helped you to take those steps? Make a separate sketch of each.
7. Lay out your life path in the room with the help of the sketches.

Put the places, animals, plants and resource person or persons in relation to the positive steps (Resource 1–3) in the past.

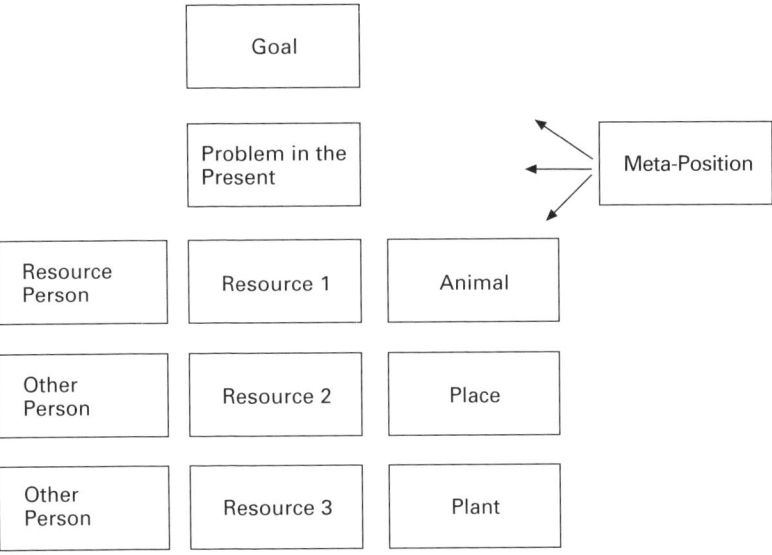

Refer to note on page 79

8. Choose a position outside the main area (meta-position) and mark it with a blank piece of paper. Stand on this paper and look at your life path from this perspective. Are the sketches in the right place? What do you notice?

9. Return to the position of the problem in the present and notice your physical and emotional reactions. How are you standing? How are you breathing? How do you feel? What are you aware of?

10. Move forwards to your goal concept and do the same thing. What differences do you notice?

11. Turn around and look back at the whole thing, particularly the "next step" that leads from the present to the resolution where you are now standing. Do you have any idea what concrete step this could be?

12. Return to the resources, moving through the present, and stand in each place in turn. How do you feel and what differences do you notice?

83

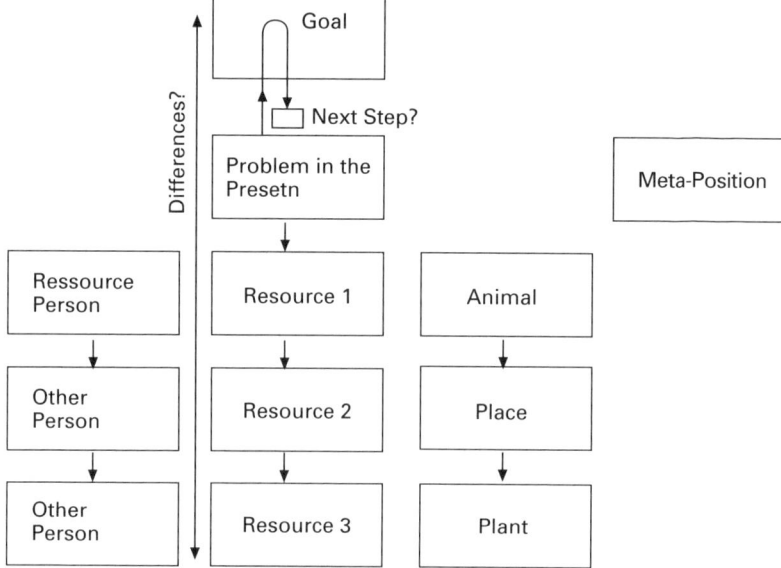

13. When you have reached the earliest resource, turn around and look at the future again. Move slowly in this direction, collecting the resource sketches as you go and taking them with you. Leave the sketch of the resource person in place.

14. Stop at the position of the problem in the present and put all of the resources underneath this paper. What has changed? How do you feel compared to how you felt earlier in this position? Is there anything new in regard to the next step?

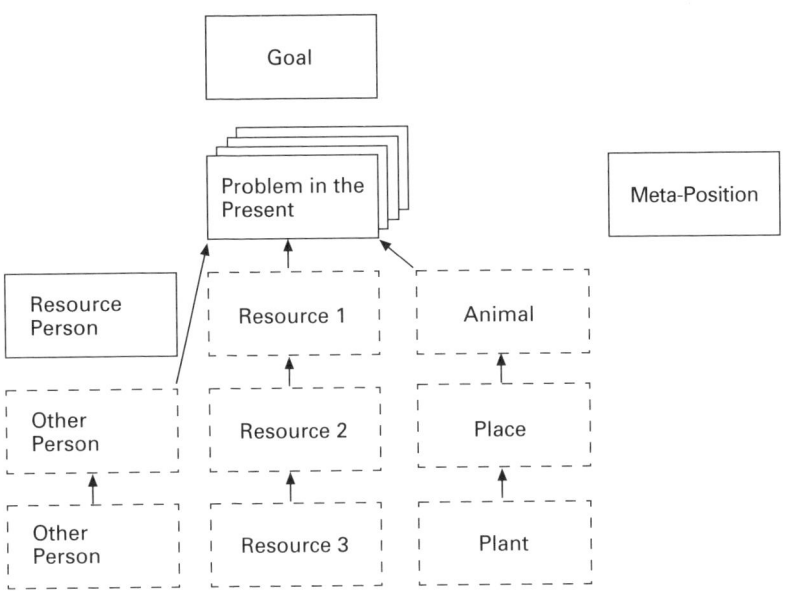

15. Bring the resource person from the past and find a place in the present for this person.

16. Stand in the position of the resource person and look through this person's eyes. Can he or she tell you anything? Carry on a dialogue with this person by changing back and forth between the two positions.

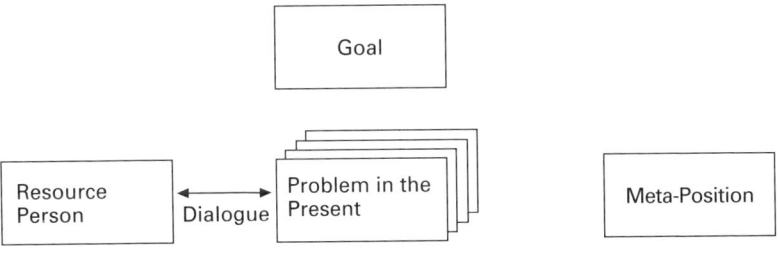

17. Return to the position of the goal, taking your resources with you, and put them underneath the sketch of the goal. Look back at the present. What concrete steps have you taken to get here? What resources have particularly helped you?

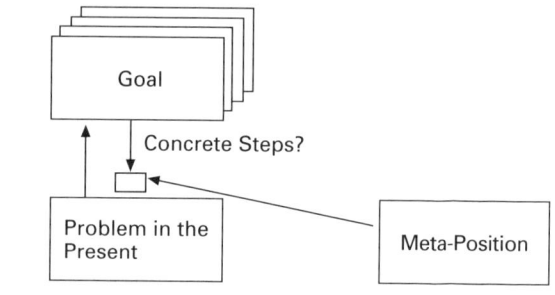

18. Step into the meta-position and look at your life path from the outside. Has it changed for you? What concrete steps can you see yourself making in the near future?
19. Carry these resources with you in some form for a while.
20. Repeat the exercise after a few months. What steps have you taken? What does your concept of the goal look like now? Has it changed? What resources have been particularly useful? What new resources have turned up? What "next steps" have emerged?

Family Image or Family Constellation as Complement to the Life Path

In the following section we will discuss how to complement the life path exercise with a representation of a family image or through a family constellation, and will look at which cases these procedures are appropriate for.

AN IMAGE OF THE FAMILY

For the sake of clarity, we distinguish between two possible ways of working with a client's relationship network. In practice, however, they frequently overlap and inter-connect. A representation of the image of the family is concerned with the biographical level, and family constellations function at the level of the archaic natural orders of relationship.

On the one hand, a representation of an image of the family can be a diagnostic tool for the therapist, since something new and different is revealed about a person in her representation of her family. The image of the family can also be used as a therapeutic element in various ways, described in the following section. In any event, a representation of a family image does not serve to resolve entanglements, in the way a family constellation may do, but rather, serves the purpose of revealing the relationships.

Seeing Family Relationships Through Other Eyes

The viewpoint of individual family members can be used to look "through other eyes" at members of the family and thus, at the whole relationship network in the family. The client is asked to draw a sketch of herself and of each member of her family of origin and is asked the question, "In what way has each person intended something good for the family?"

This question is directed towards the primary love that holds a family together. Primary love functions regardless of the quarrels, preferences, and dislikes present in every family. Additionally, the question also points to the "positive intentions" that, according to NLP, exist in every part of a system, which means every inner component, even those that seem destructive. What appears in the external family as primary love, corresponds to the "positive intentions" of each inner part (cf. p. 30).

Finally, the client lays the sketches of those involved on the floor in the places that feel right. The meta-position is laid outside the family network. The client stands in each position in turn, and experiences how differently the individual family members see the family relationships. There may also be new insights and an awareness of the positive intention of individual family members, in the sense of the NLP viewpoint that every individual piece of the system holds this intention. For example, a father's strictness, which caused the client such suffering in his childhood, may be seen quite differently from this viewpoint. Perhaps the father feared that his son would not be able to cope well with life. Looking at the family relationships in this way, using the images of the family, is also a technique appropriate for use in groups. (A detailed description of the procedure in groups is to be found on p. 118.)

Description of Procedures

1. Imagine each member of your family of origin and make a separate sketch for each of them, including yourself. Feel free to represent the individuals in any way you wish, concretely, abstractly, or even just in symbols.

2. Imagine yourself looking through the eyes of each of these people, and ask yourself the following questions:
   – In what way has each person done their best for the family?
   – What positive intentions has each had for the family?
   – Sketch a small symbol on each paper that expresses the way this person intended something good. Think about which way this person is facing, and draw a small arrow to indicate the direction.
3. Lay the papers on the floor in a way that matches your inner image of the family. Pay attention to which way each person is facing, their angles to one another, and the distances between them.
4. Lay a blank sheet of paper at a distance from the family (meta-position) and stand on this paper. Look at the picture of your family. Is each paper in the right place?

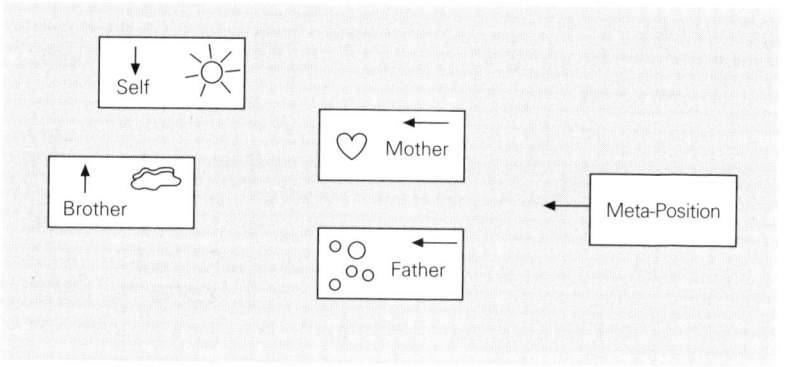

5. Stand in the position of each family member and pay attention to your physical and emotional reactions.
   – How are you standing? How are you breathing? What do you notice?
   – How does it feel to stand in this family as father, mother, or child?
   – When you look at other family members from this position, do you feel bigger, smaller, or the same size,?
   – What are the relationships between other family members like?
   – Which person is the most important?

88

6. Move to the meta-position and look at the family from the outside. Has anything changed in your perception? What have you learned? Do you have any new insights or ideas?

Representation of the Family Image Combined with Other NIG Elements

The family image can also be used to look for new possibilities for resolution within the framework of other NIG elements. If it is proving difficult to identify an appropriate concept of the goal in the work with another NIG element, and it seems as though something is missing, a family image presentation can be laid out to gain new points of view.

It is then possible to look through the eyes of another, through the eyes of other family members, at various positions along the life path, or some other NIG exercise. The client should lay out the family of origin in the form of sketches, felt pieces, or other symbols, at some distance from the exercise in progress, the life path or another element. The client is then asked to look at the life path through the eyes of individual family members. This supports a context orientation in the process and frequently provides new possibilities for resolution. Sometimes, however, the exercise reveals some family entanglement (cf. p. 45). In that case, before the appropriate next step can be found, or a solution appropriate to the exercise in progress, the entanglement will need to be resolved as described in the next section using a family constellation in an individual session or a constellation group.

The family image exercise can also be led by therapists who have not been trained in group family constellations. This work remains on the biographical level, where it is not absolutely necessary to be familiar with Hellinger's natural orders of relationship.

Description of Procedures

1. Draw a sketch of each member of your family (father, mother, siblings – including any who have died) or choose symbols or felt pieces to represent these family members. Lay the chosen spatial anchors out in the space. Add a blank paper for the meta-position.

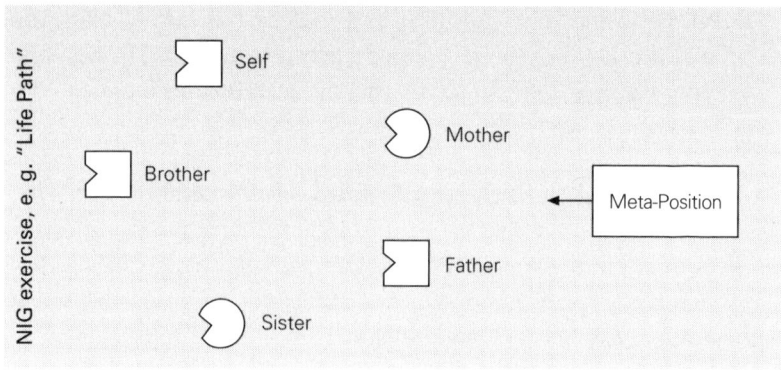

2. Stand in the position of each family member in turn and then in the meta-position. Use the meta-position viewpoint to look with different eyes at the whole picture as it is laid out. Make a new sketch of what you notice. With this new viewpoint and the sketches, return to the original NIG element and continue the work, integrating the experience with the images of the family.

Family Image – Extended Version

The representation of the family can be expanded in accordance with the intentions of the therapist and the situation of a particular client. Additional people who belong to the family system in the family of origin are: Half-brothers and sisters, their father or mother, other partners of the client's parents, parents" siblings, and grandparents. Foster parents can sometimes be included in a family image.

The current family can also be viewed from this aspect of positive intentions. The nuclear family includes a spouse, the client, and their children. Here too, an extended version is possible including other partners, and any children from those relationships.

In every family constellation, all family members, living and dead, belong to the family, and this can have major significance.

FAMILY CONSTELLATIONS

The level of the natural orders of relationships or the movements of the soul is made visible in a group using neutral representatives. A family constellation using spatial anchors is an attempt to include this level in individual therapy. In this setting we are more concerned with identifying a central entanglement and prompting a movement in the direction of resolution than we are with finding a complete picture of resolution.

Prerequisites

There are two basic pre-requisites for any decision to include a family constellation in individual therapy. The first has to do with the qualifications of the therapist. The therapist must have achieved an adequate level of personal development, advanced training, and supervision in group family constellations in order to work responsibly with constellations in individual therapy. If this is not the case and a family constellation is needed, the therapist should recommend an experienced constellation leader.

The second pre-requisite has to do with the ability of a particular client to look through the eyes of other family members to a certain degree, and the ability to look at himself from the outside as much as is possible. Most people are perfectly capable of doing this and can further develop the ability in small steps using various NIG exercises.

A serious entanglement can present real difficulties for a family constellation in individual work and a client who has never done a constellation with representatives may not be aware of the existence of such an entanglement. In a constellation group, the invisible bonds in a family become visible through the representatives of the family members. This source of information is not available in an individual setting. By standing in the positions of individual family members and noticing physical sensations, however, the client may become aware of things that were previously unavailable to him. For example, if he looks at his family through the eyes of his father or his sister, he looks at their relationship with each other from their perspective. If he looks through the eyes of his mother he can sense the difference it makes when his dead brother is in his field of vision and when he is not. This information is valuable for the client even if his awareness is not completely free of self-interests and entanglements. It is the task of an experienced constellation leader to spot those tendencies and point them out.

With intuition and experience, a therapist doing constellations in individual therapy can often find resolutions of the kind seen in

Bert Hellinger's group work, movements that go beyond merely a change of perspective.

A detailed discussion of the basic principles of family constellations is beyond the scope of this book and is widely available in other works (e. g. Hellinger 2001, Ulsamer 2003). There is also literature available on the application of family constellations in individual settings that can be recommended (Franke 2003).

At What Point in the Therapeutic Process?

In principle, family constellations can be fit into work with any NIG elements. It is particularly appropriate in the "life path", "re-imprinting", and "two sides". The addition of a family constellation is also useful when progress in the course of therapy falters because the client is caught up in secondary feelings, such as rage or blaming (cf. p. 42). A constellation can also bring resolution when a traumatic memory connected to a family member comes up in the course of an NIG exercise and strong emotions take over. Likewise, the systemic-phenomenological view of the family can be very useful when the client or the therapist has the impression that there is something or someone else needed in order to find a good resolution. Similarly, a client may not be able to take in, or unconsciously sabotages, solutions and goals that seem reasonable and worthwhile. He needs to look at whether his goal is in harmony with his family, or if he might need the blessing of some family member, or if there could be an identification with some earlier family member, perhaps someone who carried some guilt.

Typical Objections and Questions

The therapist will recognize the right moment to include a family constellation by noticing particular objections or questions from the client. "Actually, everything is quite clear to me and I know what I could do, but I don't do it." Or, "Everything is going well now, but I am afraid that will soon change." Such comments from a client raise the suspicion that the family relationship network is hindering a solution at the biographical level and a family constellation would be the next therapeutic step (cf. case study: *The Positive Intentions of the Symptoms, or Stress as a Helper,* p. 154).

When a family constellation seems advisable from a therapeutic point of view, it can be put directly into the NIG exercise currently in progress. If this is impossible due to time considerations, the therapist can keep it in mind and pick it up again at an opportune moment in the next session.

What Information is Necessary?

As with constellations in a group setting, it is not relevant for a client to get into information about the character of family members, nor interpretations of events. Instead, the therapist asks about the existence of siblings, half-siblings, prior relationships of the parents, and possibly about excluded family members such as aborted or stillborn children, or missing or rejected family members. The other central question is, "What has happened?" This concerns events that have affected the entire family: Early deaths, exile, political entanglements, strong church affiliations, emigration, etc.

Choice of People

It is always advisable to begin a constellation with as few people as possible. The choice is made according to the client's response to questions about important events that have affected the whole family. Family members that the client does not know, for example an uncle who emigrated or one who died in the war, are often particularly relevant. A beloved Grandma, who the client may have mentioned first, in all probability has nothing to do with the entanglement. She may be a potential resource person who can provide access to primary love inaccessible to the client with her own parents. Missing family members are particularly relevant in the attempt to uncover entanglements and should be represented. Completing the family picture is often an important step towards resolution.

In very complex dynamics, with many family members involved or family events that are hidden, a family constellation in a group with representatives is to be recommended. Collective issues such as war, persecution, or people driven from their homes are more appropriately handled within the energy field of a group.

Examples of Possible Applications

Ms Schultheiss is seeking a new professional direction after many years devoted to raising her children. She works on this theme using the life path exercise. In looking for resources for a new start, she remembers joyfully the birth of her first child and makes a sketch of this. When she stands on this paper, her joy turns to grief and she begins to cry. From the meta-position, Ms Schultheiss reports that this child was not her first child at all, because she had lost her first child through a miscarriage. Since this child was never properly mourned, the therapist asks Ms Schultheiss to lay out her present family with anchors in a separate area. In this constellation, Ms Schultheiss is able to grieve for her lost child and give her living children their correct place in the line of siblings. At a later time she addresses the issue of her professional new start with the help of NIG.

In her marriage, Ms Bergmann has always accommodated herself to the wishes and expectations of her husband. Having determined that this is not good for her in the long run, she would like to learn to be more aware of her own needs and be able to communicate them to her husband. The therapist accompanies her through the NIG exercise "developing skills". In this exercise the focus is on using capabilities developed in the past to achieve a desired skill in the future. The exercise proceeds very satisfactorily for Ms Bergmann, but finally, as she is standing on her desired skill, padded with resources, she feels anticipatory happiness and confidence but also an emptiness on her left side. In answer to the therapist's question about her mother, Ms Bergmann says that, exactly as herself, her mother always put her own needs off to the side. In the constellation that follows, Ms Bergmann stands opposite her mother and bows in respect to her mother's achievements in raising four children alone during and after the war (her father returned much later from a prisoner of war camp). She says to her mother, "Now I can see it. You couldn't possibly have thought of yourself". As she then stands in the position of her mother, she can feel how happy her mother is that her daughter has a chance, in these different times, to pay attention to her own needs. Ms Bergmann lays the sketch of herself on top of the desired skill and the sketch of her mother behind her. As she stands in her own position, with the desired skill underneath her, her mother's blessing and strength behind her gives her a warm and joyful feeling.

Description of Procedures: Family Constellations

Family constellations, as described here, may be the main intervention in one or more sessions or the therapist may decide in the middle of an NIG exercise to suggest a constellation of the client's family. From information gained in the initial interview, and the client's reactions during the exercise, the therapist develops a hypothesis about possible family entanglements. He is guided by this hypothesis, his intuition, and his experience in leading the client through a family constellation.

Instructions to the Client
1. Make a sketch for each person needed, including yourself, or use the drawings already on hand, or other symbols. Place each paper in a place that seems right, inside or outside of the configuration we have already done. Mark a place with a blank sheet of paper or a symbol for the meta-position (neutral observer, or another term).
2. Move between your own position and that of each other person in your family. What is your physical and emotional reaction when you feel, for example, like your father or mother in this relationship network? Pay attention to the direction that each person is facing. Is the person looking off into the distance, at the floor, or at another person? How do the family members react to one another? What relationship structures become clear?
3. In between times, return to the meta-position and take in the whole relationship network from the outside. What changes when you have looked through the eyes of other family members?
4. Are there any other people in your family that you feel are missing?

The therapist has to decide how far a client is able to go in this process, and is guided by the client's spontaneous reactions and feelings while standing in the various positions of the family members. The therapist tests out his hypothesis and broadens his knowledge of the dynamics in this family. The question is what might lead out of the entanglement in the direction of a resolution. The process might involve changing the positions of the sketches, adding additional family members, speaking sentences of resolution, or a ritual that allows the client to engage in the process. What is demanded of the therapist, besides intuition, is a precise understanding of the dynamics of entanglements. Such knowledge and understanding can only be acquired in Hellinger-style constellation groups.

The therapist can bring the family constellation to a close when a movement towards resolution has begun. Just as in constellation work in a group, it is also true here that the constellation should be concluded when the energy is at its high point. This means the point at which the reactions of the client indicate that an inner process has been set in motion. No additional interventions are made to try to improve things.

If the constellation has been used as a complement to one of the NIG elements, the client returns to the interrupted exercise, taking with her the results of the constellation as a source of strength. She will have a feeling about how and if the sketches from the constellation should be integrated in the configuration of sketches from the other NIG exercise. If time allows, the NIG exercise can be continued in the same session. If not, that element can be taken up again in a later session.

A Family Constellation and Life Path: The Core of NIG

Although family constellations, as described above, are complementary to all NIG elements or can be used alone, experience has shown that in practice, the combination of the life path exercise and a family constellation form the core of NIG. The life path exemplifies the resource and context orientation of the biographical level. The family constellation represents the level of the orders of relationships in the therapeutic process (cf. p. 29); created reality and manifested reality are both included in a complementary way (cf. p. 23).

Work with the life path has to do with very concrete steps in daily life. A family constellation, on the other hand, brings about an inner attitude of respect for the life network one has been born into. This inner attitude is expressed primarily in respect and love for one's parents. If that is impossible, then there may at least be an acceptance of them.

In many cases it is enough to simply allow the results of the constellation to work their effects and wait to see if and what next steps emerge from this altered inner state. There are also situations, however, in which the client is depending on concrete solutions to a problem. Then it is a good idea to supplement the work with the life path exercise or another therapeutic element, as described.

Re-Imprinting and Changing the View of Past Trauma

The NIG element of re-imprinting is concerned with traumatic experience in the past, as opposed to the life path exercise, where the primary focus is on the search for resources. In addition, this exercise represents an interface between family constellations and NLP. The book *NLP und das Familien-Stellen* [NLP and Family Constellations] (Stresius, Castella, u. Grochowiak 2001) describes this interface and its therapeutic applications.

Imprinting means leaving a mark, an indelible influence. Re-imprinting, an NLP procedure developed by Robert Dilts (Dilts, Halbom a. Smith 1990), is essentially a procedure for making a new mark, a new impression. Using re-imprinting, beliefs formed by traumatic experiences in the past are re-worked to become congruent with the current, different situation. This new impression allows for an altered view of the past, present, and future. As opposed to Dilt's version, the NIG version of re-imprinting is more systemically orientated and has been modified by the introduction of the figure of the "old person".

Leaving the present problem and the image of a good solution, the client looks for an experience that seems to be a source of the current problem. She goes back to the relationship system of that time, and tries to look at the situation from the viewpoint of the imprinting person, that is, the person centrally involved in the traumatic experience. She begins to experience her own positive intentions as well as the positive intentions of the imprinting person in the past, and begins to alter her viewpoint. In this way, old beliefs can be dissolved and new beliefs developed that are more appropriate to the current situation. She is supported in this by the neutral observer (meta-position) standing outside the events, and the mature, wise, old person that she will someday become. The insights gained in this process are then used in the search for solutions in the future.

Re-Imprinting is not only useful for working through traumatic memories from childhood; it can also provide access to systemic connections. For example, an interrupted reaching-out movement of a child may have been caused by the child's long stay in hospital, but also by her mother's inner withdrawal, which in turn was perhaps caused perhaps by her early loss of her own mother. If, based on information from the interview, the therapist sees indications of such possible entanglements in connection with the problem, systemic orientated re-imprinting is the tool of choice. If a family constellation in a group seems more appropriate for the client, re-imprinting can be used either as preparation for the constellation or as a follow-up method afterwards.

Description of Procedures: Basic Structure: Re-Imprinting

1. What is the problem and what is your concept of a good solution? (See goal criteria, p. 78)
2. Make three sketches with your non-dominant hand:
   - A sketch of your present including the problem.
   - A sketch of a state in the future in which this problem has been solved
     or has changed in such a way that you can deal with it yourself.
   - A picture of the old person that you will someday become.
3. Lay the sketches out in the room.
4. Mark a place outside the configuration (meta-position: neutral observer).

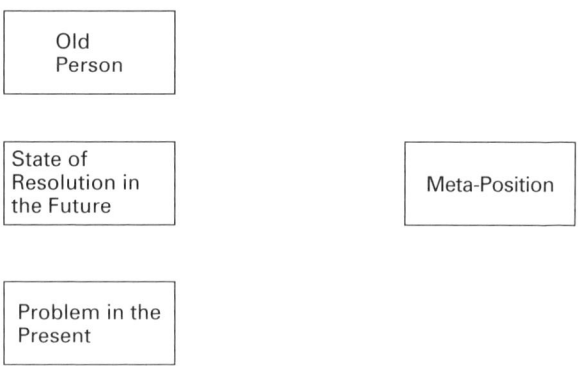

Relevant Note on p. 79

5. Stand in the position of the problem in the present and notice your physical and emotional reaction. How are you standing? How are you breathing? How do you feel? What do you notice?

98

6. Go to the state of resolution in the future and do the same.
7. Remember back through your life until you come to a place where memories arise that could be a cause of your current problem. How do you feel there? Who was the person of influence for you at that time? Where is that person standing: In front of you, next to you, or behind you? Make a sketch of the child you were at that time. Make another sketch of the influential person and lay both sketches wherever it feels right to you.

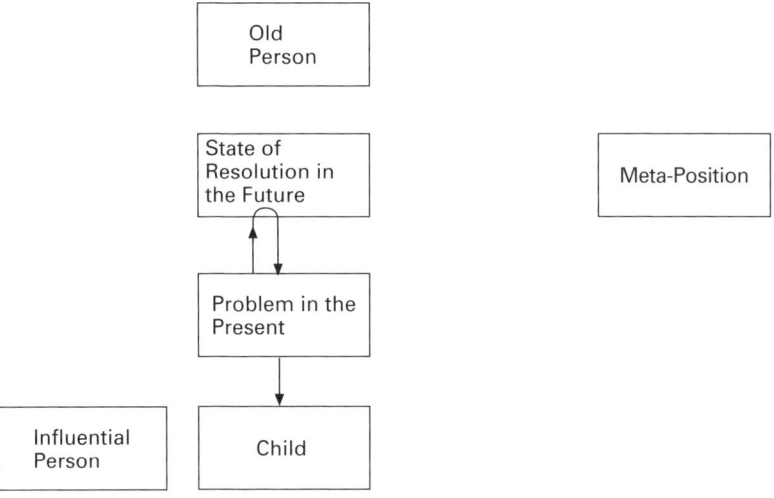

8. Alternate between the position of the child and the position of the influential person. How do you feel in each position? How does the influential person react to the child? How does the child react to the influential person? What beliefs does the child hold? What beliefs does the influential person hold?
9. Stand in the meta-position and look at the influential person and the child from the outside. What is the positive intention of each?
10. Move to the position of the old person and look at the influential person and the child. What is the positive intention of each from this viewpoint?
11. Alternate between the position of the child and that of the influential person. What positive intentions are you aware of in each?

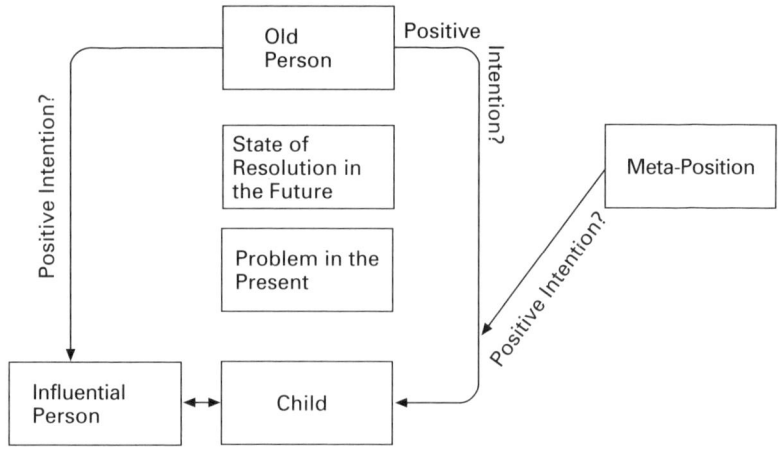

12. Return to the position of the present adult with the problem. What has changed? What insights do you have? What possible courses of action have emerged? What steps can you see yourself making in the direction of a solution?

13. Move slowly back to the position of the state of resolution in the future. Look back again. How do you feel? When you look at the space-time distance to the problem in the present, does it seem right to you? Too large or too small? What concrete steps have you taken to get from that problem to here, a place of resolution?

14. Go back to the meta-position or the position of the old person. From this viewpoint, what concrete steps can you see yourself making?

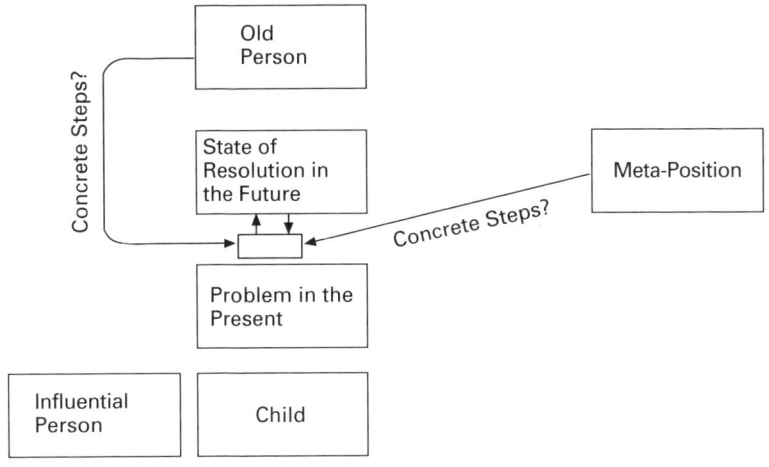

Basic Information about Re-Imprinting and Family Constellations

The process of the re-imprinting exercise frequently contains a mini-constellation because of the inclusion of the client as a child and the influential person from the past. Usually the influential person is a parent, sibling, or other close relative. The way this is handled depends on many factors: The client and his issue, previous experience, and the focus of the therapist.

In the basic structure of re-imprinting as described in the previous section, the client's change of viewpoint is brought about in a systemic-constructivist way, through dialogues between the involved parties and by looking for positive intentions. Re-imprinting and family constellations, used together, function as in systemic-phenomenology, with the client turning towards the family. By changing the position of the sketches or adding further family members, previously unrecognized family dynamics and entanglements may be revealed. Recognizing and acknowledging these dynamics may bring great relief to the client. It is often possible to also find healing sentences that the client can take from the past and carry with him into the future. These healing sentences serve as resources as the person looks forward into the future at a state where the problem is resolved, or has changed so that he can deal with it himself.

Case Example of Re-Imprinting and a Family Constellation

Mr Miltner considers his father and his very strict upbringing to be the cause of his current problems. Mr M, or rather, Mr M as the child he used to be, makes contact with his father in the procedure described in the previous section. It becomes clear that the father is unavailable for his child and the child turns away in resignation. At this point the therapist decides to move into a family constellation. She asks Mr M what happened in his father's life and learns that his father's father never returned from the war. The therapist asks the client to make a sketch of his grandfather and to lay the sketch with his sketches of himself and of his father. Moving back and forth between the three positions, it is clear to Mr M how strongly the early death of his grandfather influenced the relationship between his father and himself. He is able to say to his father, "I can see your pain now," and can acknowledge the fate of his father and his grandfather. Following the sentence of resolution, Mr M and his father look at one other with love and caring. Mr M turns to his problem in the present with a different feeling, strengthened by his father and grandfather.

Description of Procedures: Re-Imprinting and Family Constellations

1. What is the problem and what is your concept of a good solution? (See goal criteria, p. 78)
2. Sketch with your non-dominant hand
   - An image of the present including the problem
   - An image of a state in the future in which this problem has been resolved or changed in such a way that you can deal with it yourself.
3. Lay the sketches out on the floor.
4. Find a position outside the configuration of the two sketches

State of Resolution in the Future	Meta-Position

Problem in the Present

See note, p. 79

5. Stand in the position of the problem in the present and pay attention to your physical and emotional reactions. How are you standing? How are you breathing? How do you feel? What do you notice?
6. Now stand in the position of the state of resolution in the future and do the same.
7. Go back through time until you come to a place where a memory comes up that seems to you to be a cause of your current problem. How do you feel there? Who in your family (present family or family of origin) is associated with this problem? Where is this person standing: In front of you, next to you, or behind you?
   – Make a sketch of the child, or younger person you were at that time
     (for simplicity's sake, this person will be called "child").
   – Make another sketch of the person in your family and place the two sketches where it feels right.

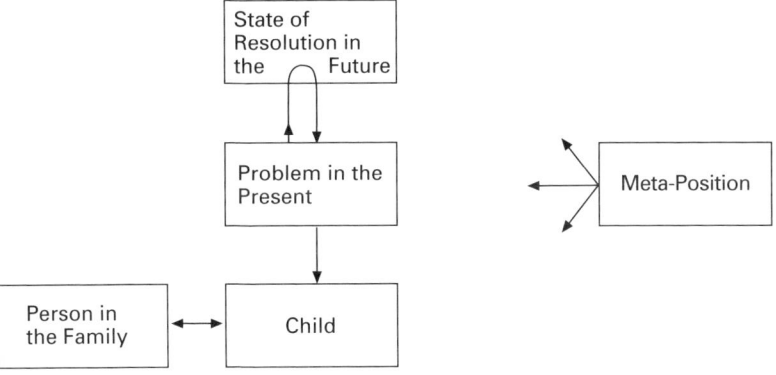

8. Alternate between the position of the child and the position of the person in your family. How does one feel and how does the other one feel? Let them make contact with one another. How do they react to each other?
9. Stand in the meta-position and look at the scene from the outside.
10. If necessary, at this point you can continue with a family constellation and possibly add one or more family members (cf. p. 101).

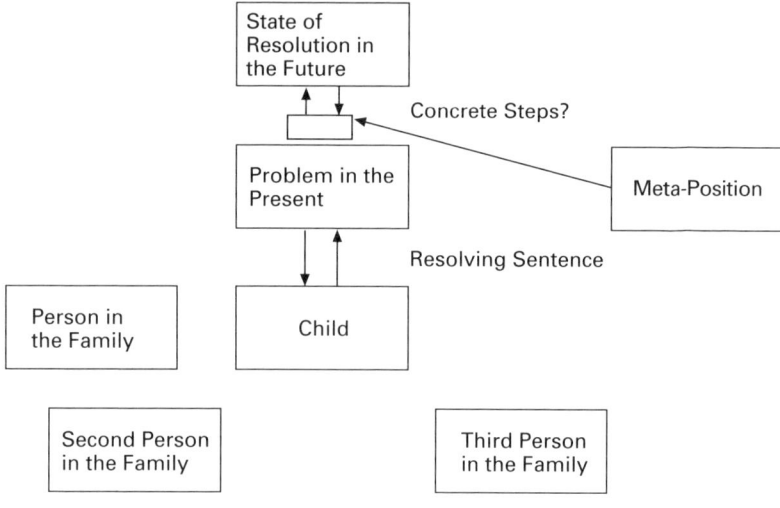

11. Return to the position of the problem in the present and notice any changes. If you have found a resolving sentence, repeat it while looking back at the past occurrence in the family.

12. Turn and move slowly to the position of a state of resolution in the future. Look back again.
    How does the space/time distance to the problem in the present seem to you? Is it just right, too large, or too small? What concrete steps have you taken to get from the problem to the resolution?

13. Go back to the meta-position: From this viewpoint, what concrete next steps can you see yourself making?

Additional Exercise: Healing the Inner Child

When the client has made contact with the child of the past in the reimprinting exercise, the experience can be deepened and intensified through an exercise from Erika Chopich, called "Healing the Inner Child" (Chopich and Paul 1997). It also works well in groups or as a self-help exercise.

The exercise is particularly effective if it is continued over a longer period of time to establish the contact with the inner child as habitual. As a rule, the inner child is felt in everyday life as a feeling of things not being quite right, tiredness, anxiety, sorrow, shyness, or disappointment. When one of these feelings arises, if one pays attention to it in a way that takes the needs of the inner child into consideration, it has fulfilled its purpose and can disappear.

1. Relax and surrender to the inhale and exhale of your own breathing. Imagine a safe place that gives you strength and where you feel well.
2. Make contact with the hurt child, that used to be and represent this child in a coloured sketch.
3. Consciously relax again, welcome your inner child, and talk to him or her in the following way.
   - The caring adult/I writes questions with the dominant hand
   - The inner child answers, using the non-dominant hand
   You can use a different pen, or a different colour for each hand.
4. Ask your inner child the following questions,
   - Who are you?
   - How do you feel?
   - Why do you feel that way?
   - What can I do for you?
5. In answer to the last question, share with your inner child exactly what you can do concretely to meet his or her needs. Do not make any empty promises!
6. Agree on a time to meet again.
   Thank your inner child for coming and say goodbye.

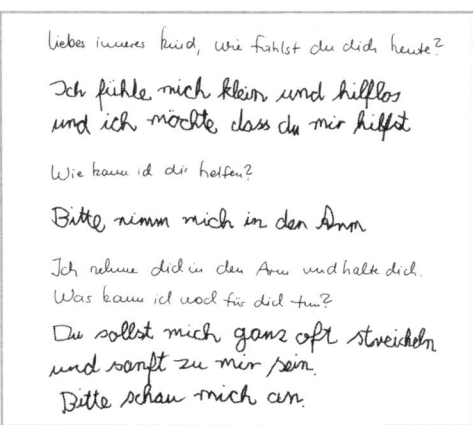

Dear inner child, how are you feeling today?
I feel little and helpless and I want you to help me.
How can I help you?
Please take me in your arms.
I take you in my arms and hold you.
What else can I do for you?
You should stroke me a lot and be very gentle with me.
Please look at me.

Two Sides

Ambivalence: The Inability to Make Decisions

Ambivalence is the inability to make decisions or swinging indecisively back and forth between two possibilities. This is a problem that may prompt someone to seek counselling.

There are differing solutions to dealing with ambivalence. The decision may come down in favour of one of the two possibilities, a synthesis may be found that combines the two possibilities, a previously unseen solution might emerge, or the polarity may simply remain until a resolution develops at some point in the future. What they all have in common, however, is that a solution is only functional when the positive intention of both parts is seen and acknowledged, even if one of the two seems self-destructive or destructive in some other way.

Inner Divisions as Two Sides of the Same Coin

If the client's problem is not ambivalence, but is rather, for example, the necessity of changing some behaviour (for instance, resisting eating binges, or stopping quarrelsome, provoking behaviour with a partner), the therapist or counsellor can easily work with it as a "two sides" situation. De Shazer asks, "When is it better?" Or, "When and where do you not have this problem?" The answer to this question reveals the inner part that already knows the solution. The part that is stuck in the problem is usually more present to the client. To continue the procedure, each side is sketched on a separate piece of paper and used in the NIG element described below.

The Shadow

One side is often experienced as being light, bright, and appealing, whereas the other is represented as black, terrifying, and repellent. As the saying goes, "Where there is a lot of light, there is also a lot of shadow." Certainly since C. G. Jung's work we have been aware of the strength that can be developed by integrating our dark, rejected side. Those who are able to accept their light and their dark sides as parts of the "paradoxical structure of the soul" (cf. p. 186), have a special strength and aura about them. Working out the positive intentions of the dark side and taking them in can be a step along this way.

Dialogue between the Inner Divisions

The description of the procedures for the "two sides" exercise is a good example of how, in systemic therapy, the resolution of inner conflicts is sought in a dialogue between seemingly intractable polarities. The task is always to let each side have its say. When acknowledgement and honour are accorded the positive intentions that each side has for the whole, the common features of the two sides in this regard are easier to develop.

The description of the procedure for this exercise in the following section ends with an exercise taken from de Shazer involving observation and prediction. This exercise assumes that in the course of time a solution will emerge by itself. The procedure opens up for the "autonomy of the unconscious" (Robert Dilts), and is useful when the next, concrete steps are not yet directly apparent.

Following this description, there is a variation in which a concrete next step can be considered. Sometimes the common features that are discovered carry the solution within them and the client can turn his attention to the next concrete step towards a solution.

Description of Procedure: Basic Structure: "Two Sides"

1. Imagine the two inner parts of yourself that are involved. If possible, try to visualize a picture of each.
2. Make a sketch of each with your non-dominant hand.
3. Lay out the two pieces of paper in the room and mark a place with a blank piece of paper at an appropriate distance for the meta-position (neutral observer).

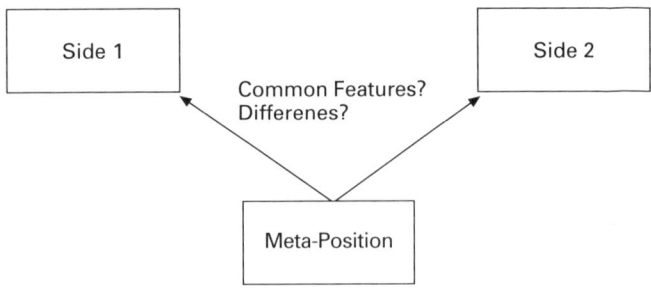

4. Stand in the meta-position and look at the whole picture.
   - How do you experience the two sides from this position?
   - What differences and what common features do you notice?
5. Move to one of the two sides and pay attention to your physical and emotional reaction. How are you standing? How are you breathing? How do you feel? What do you notice? Change to the other side and do the same.
6. Return to the meta-position and look at both sides again.
   - Is there any difference between how you see them now compared to how
     you saw them before?
   - In what situations or with whom is each side problematic?
   - In what situations or with whom is each side helpful?

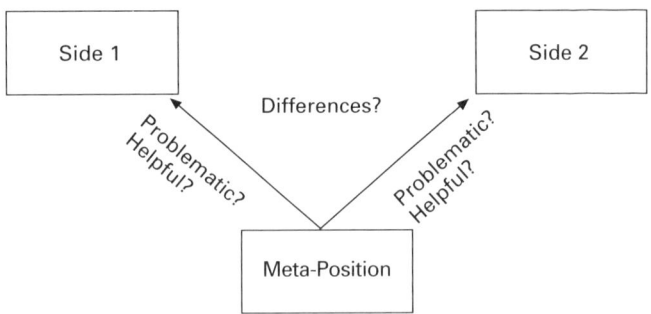

7. Stand on one side again and look over at the other side. Tell the other side what your positive intentions are. Do the same from the other side. Let the two sides carry on a dialogue, alternating positions, sharing positive intentions, and noticing the reactions of the other side.

8. Go back to the meta-position. How do you see the whole picture now? What have you found out about the positive intentions of each side? What concrete possibilities have emerged?

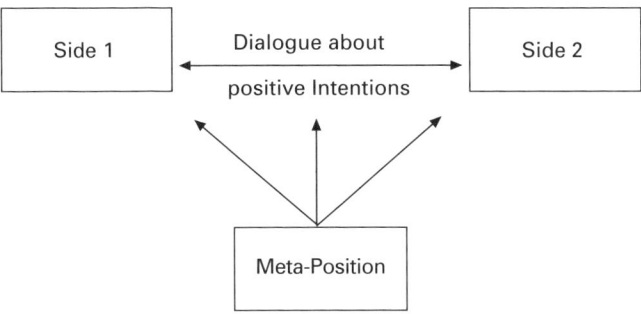

9. Additional exercise: Use the two sketches to look back at the end of each day to see when and where one particular side was in the foreground and what effects that has on you and your environment. Expand the sketches or draw new ones whenever one or both sides have changed in some essential way. Imagine the next day and make a prediction as to how the next day will look in terms of this interplay between the two sides. Make a note of your prediction and repeat this process for a few days, comparing your predictions to your observations of what actually happens during the day. What changes as you do this?

Description of Procedures: Two Sides – Extended Version
Follow steps one to eight as described above.

9. Add a symbol to each sketch representing the positive intentions of each side.

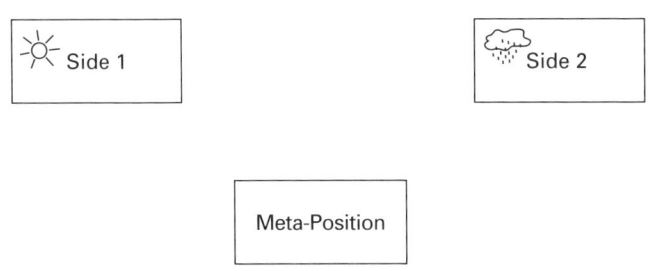

10. Return to the meta-position and look at the whole picture.
    − What do the two sides have in common in terms of positive intentions?
    − Make a sketch representing these common features. Put the sketch on the floor and imagine that out of these common features, a state develops in the future in which the conflict between the two sides is resolved or so changed that you do not experience it as a problem anymore.

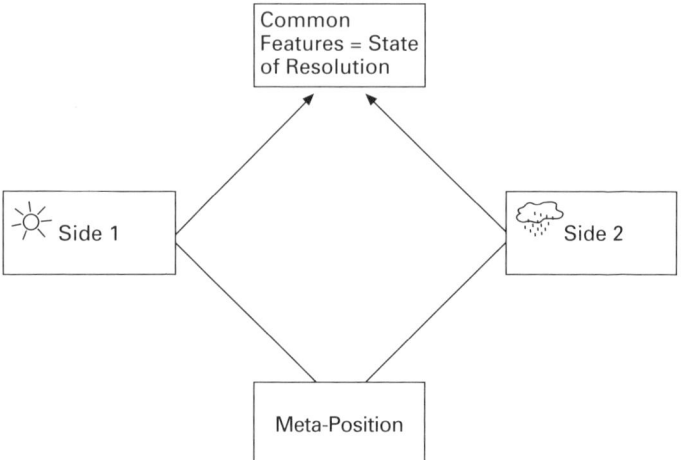

11. Stand on the sketch of the state of resolution and notice your physical   and emotional reactions. How are you standing? How are you breathing? How do you feel? What do you notice? Look back at the two sides of your present situation. Which concrete next steps can you see yourself making from the present to the state of resolution?

12. Return to each of the two sides in the present in turn and look at the state of resolution. What concrete next steps in the direction of a solution come to mind?

13. Stand in the meta-position and look at the whole from the outside. Is the spatial relationship still right? What next step in the direction of a solution would you advise from this position? Would the neutral observer like to share any insights or observations?

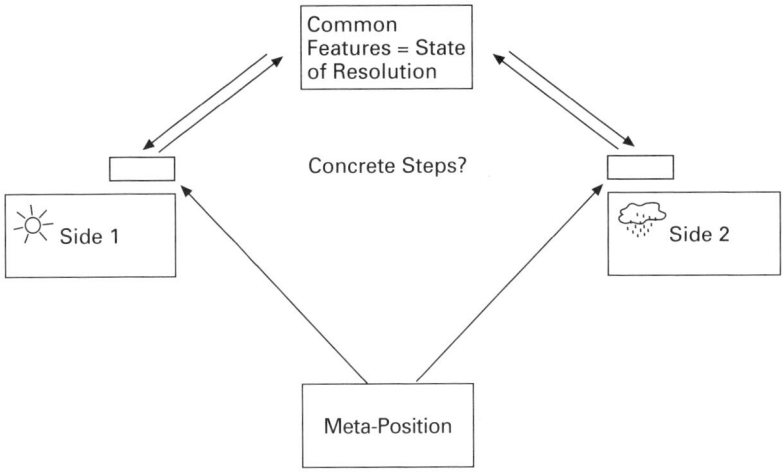

"Two Sides" as Phases on the Life Path

If the therapist has the suspicion that one or both of the internal divisions have something to do with a phase or experience of childhood, the client can be asked, "How old is this part?" and "How old is the other part?" If the client can name one or two different ages, it would suggest that a life path should be developed. It is important that the resource qualities for *both* sides are worked out, for example, through positive intentions.

A sketch of the present is completed in which the two parts are represented in their relationship to one another. A sketch is drawn of the state of resolution in the future in which the client needs no more counselling. The client lays out the new sketches with the sketches of the two sides, which now symbolize two phases of development in the past. If this is successful, the life path exercise can be concluded as described on page 78. If it is not satisfactory, possibly "re-imprinting" or a family constellation is called for.

Inner Divisions in Systemic Terms

We have previously said that the "inner family", the inner characteristics of a person, frequently has a relationship to the external family of origin. (cf. p. 30). In the work with two sides, it may appear that one or both sides have a close connection to entangled family members (cf. case study p. 149). As previously described, a mini-constellation could be put into the session as it is in the re-imprinting exercise, and then return to the work with the two sides continued. Or, you might move completely to a family constellation at this point.

In a constellation using representatives it is also possible to begin with inner characteristics. For example, one representative takes the part of the person that knows the solution, another represents the part that is hindering a solution, and a third is chosen to represent the client (the "I" or the focus). The client sets up the constellation as usual, and the representatives are asked for feedback. From this verbal feedback and the spontaneous movements of the representatives, a systemic connection will usually appear. The constellation can be expanded to include the family members who are relevant to the entanglement (cf. case study p. 159). To proceed in this way, the leader needs to be competent at working with movements of the soul in groups.

Allowing Polarities to Remain

Regardless of which procedure has been chosen for the work with the two sides, the process may fail to move forward to resolution. An intervention that is often very effective in such cases is to let the polarities of the two sides stand as they are. New information from the work alters the previous way of seeing things and sometimes confuses things initially, and it takes some time to integrate this information into the whole. If the subject is taken up again at a later date, it is quite possible that, with this new stimulation, movement towards a solution will have developed in one direction or another, or perhaps even a new, third possibility will emerge.

HOMEWORK

Homework tasks are suggested to help the client test out and ground new behaviour patterns. They are meant to counteract the client's possible belief that they have already exhausted all their behavioural resources for solving this problem (from Schlippe and Schweitzer 2002). For instance, in NIG work, if the client has found recommendations for a change in behaviour or the next steps towards the goal, these can be implemented through homework tasks. Relatively brief exercises, reinforce the experience of being able to change a mental state through one's own efforts (de Shazer 1988).

Observing and Predicting

The NIG version of de Shazer's prediction exercise (de Shazer 1988). described in the next section has proved itself many times over in practice. The two sketches of inner characteristics from the NIG element of the two sides can be used for this homework task. Two inner parts that have become clear during discussion with a client can be sketched: The part that represents the problem, and the part that knows the solution. The "solution" part should not be just a fantasy, but rather, is something that has been present at some point, somewhere along the life path. It can be located, for example, with the questions, "When or where are things better?" "When or where were things better?" "Describe the inner part of yourself that makes that possible." It is helpful to look at a relatively short period of time, perhaps one day, or one week, and also to notice shorter periods of time during which the solution part has moved into the foreground.

When the "problem part" and the "solution part" have been identified and sketched, the therapist suggests that before going to sleep at night, the client lay out the two sketches and check whether anything has changed in the meantime. "If so, then draw new sketches. Look back at the day just completed day and remember when and where each part was in the foreground determining your feelings and behaviour. Make a note of this. Make a prediction about how the two parts will move between foreground and background tomorrow and note this down. Bring the papers to the next session." The therapist includes the result of this homework task in the next session.

This exercise works in many cases as an indirect suggestion in the direction of improvement. The client also gains insight and a feeling for the context connection of his problem. Frequently, the part of the person with the solution moves into the foreground without the client consciously trying to change something. The exercise is therefore very appropriate as a self-help exercise.

Surprises

"Do something completely different!" (from Schlippe and Schweitzer 2002). Behave in a way that is different than usual. Surprise yourself or others daily with some new and unusual behaviour. Write down the new behaviour and its effect.

Continuing to Draw on Your Own

From time to time, lay out your papers, look at them, and stand on them. Are you aware of any changes in the meantime? If yes, lay the papers out and change the distance between them, or add new sketches. The new drawings might add further resources or resource persons, an altered concept of the goal, a change in the next concrete steps towards the goal, or a new alternative behaviour. What effect does the new drawing have on the whole?

7. Applications of Neuro-Imaginative Gestalting

NIG in Individual Therapy and Counselling with Adults

Since NIG is primarily a tool for individual therapy, the most important aspects of this topic have already been presented. For consulting in companies or institutions, it should be noted here that at the start of the work, you can forgo the creation of sketches for floor markers and instead use prepared symbols such as different coloured circles and rectangles, or materials appropriate to the setting. In the course of the work, if it suits the context, you can explain that the left-handed sketch is a professional technique to communicate with the right half of the brain, which looks at the whole picture and therefore increases the effectiveness of the work. It is also advisable to be cautious about any use of rituals, such as bowing down or speaking standard sentences, which might provoke a negative reaction in people who have not come to you for therapy. Otherwise, what is written later in the section on supervision is also valid in these situations.

NIG with Children

As already mentioned in chapter 5, Neuro-Imaginative Gestalting is suitable for work with children if the individual NIG exercises are introduced in a manner appropriate for children and the procedures simplified.

Children younger than ten or twelve are still primarily kinaesthetically orientated in their awareness and expression. If they are asked how they are feeling, the verbal answers are more often than not monosyllabic. Asked to draw a picture, however, the response is immediate and enthusiastic. In their drawings, children spontaneously express their situation, their environment, and their goals, sometimes very dramatically.

The back and forth movement between the sketches also speaks to the child's kinaesthetic style. Standing on a sketch, most children are clearly aware of any physical changes. The verbal communications about awareness are perhaps not as differentiated, but the sentence, "I want to go away from here," or "It is good here;" transmits an unmistakably clear message. Children are often happy to display their "work" at home and so continue to live with a topic for a while in this way. Sometimes they also bring further drawings to a later session.

The sketches can be used in many ways with children in individual and group therapy as well as in the field of education, in learning therapy, and parent-child counselling.

NIG in Couples Therapy

The NIG elements of the life path and the image of the family, as well as family constellations can be successfully incorporated in couples therapy. For example, each partner can lay out their life path separately, and take note of parallel or divergent tendencies. Do their concepts of the goal have something in common? What do the goal concepts of one partner mean to the other? Do the representations of the problem situation in the present correspond or are there differences? Are the resources a source of connection or do they push the partners apart? Is there a next step that would be appropriate for both partners?

The exercise with two sides is also useful in couple therapy. For example, with a couple who are ambivalent about whether to marry at this time or not, one partner can sketch both scenarios, and the other partner is asked to sketch how he or she sees the two representations of the first partner. The sketches are laid out in the room, giving each the opportunity to see himself or herself through the eyes of the other partner. This provides a new perspective on the qualities of the relationship. Therapeutic creativity is called for to help the process to a conclusion that includes both partners.

NIG as a Self-Help Tool

It is possible to use NIG as a tool to help oneself in crisis situations. Most of the NIG elements are largely self- contained procedures and the function of the therapist is mainly to accompany the client. Through the techniques of sketching with the non-dominant hand, noticing physical reactions, looking through the eyes of another, and gaining objectivity about oneself and the problem from the meta-position, a dialogue with the unconscious occurs that, under certain circumstances, makes the presence of a helper superfluous (cf. p. 41). A trusted person to read the descriptions of procedures aloud may be helpful and certainly helps maintain concentration.

As depicted in the description of procedures, the life path exercise can be repeated alone after a period of time to take stock of what has happened in the meantime and, if need be, to make adjustments in the concepts of goals and solutions to suit the current situation. There may also be new resources to be added. Other NIG elements that are suitable for self-help are the "two sides", "developing skills", and possibly also "interrupting patterns". The exercises that are not suitable for self-help are the extended version of "re-imprinting" and family constellations. These elements require the eye of an experienced and intuitive helper that cannot be replaced by a dialogue with one's own unconscious. This is not the case with the family image if the positions of the family members are used only as a point of view, and not as an attempt to uncover entanglements or to find resolutions. We are aware, of course, that despite this warning (or perhaps because of it), some people will surely go ahead and try it anyway!

NIG IN A GROUP SETTING

Bringing In Various NIG Elements

In principle, all the elements of NIG detailed in chapter 6 can be used in groups as well as in an individual setting. In this case, the instructions are written as given by the group leader to everyone in the group simultaneously. The procedure and organization for this is easy. The leader should formulate the instructions clearly and simplify the assignments so that only the sketches that are absolutely necessary are drawn and laid out. To begin with, it is advisable to choose one particular aspect of an exercise and practise with it, for example, the effect of the meta-position, or working out appropriate goals.

In group work, just as in individual work, the emphasis in on a creative use of the individual NIG elements. With growing experience, a group leader can more easily adapt NIG elements to suit the needs and goals of a particular group.

Working with the meta-position is a simple and rewarding exercise as it acquaints the members of the group with the astounding effects gained by looking in from the outside. By changing perspective it is possible to see not only one's own problems in a different light, but also the reasons for movement and the inner logic of other people and systems. The meta-position can be used in therapy and personal growth work, but also in advanced training, coaching, and consulting. The same is true of the exercise "interrupting patterns". Here too, the focus is on a change of perspective and the resulting recommendations for changes in behaviour.

The life path exercise in a simplified form is appropriate in a group for working on personal goals as well as professional or specialized goal setting. The resources should be reduced to allow for a clear overview of the process.

If the life path exercise in its complete form seems too cumbersome for use in a specific group situation, you can focus on one aspect, for example, the concept of an appropriate goal. In this case, the criteria for an appropriate goal are discussed and worked out together, and the goal is sketched and tested out by standing in that position and then changing perspectives.

The following section contains examples of instructions for Neuro-Imaginativ e Gestalting in a group.

Image of the Family

This exercise provides a way for every participant in a group to individually get in touch with their own personal family of origin. The focus is on being aware of the relationships in the family from various perspectives, which may result in a change in people's way of seeing their families.

During the first phase, the whole group does a relaxation exercise so the participants can establish contact with their core family members (biological father, biological mother, child). In an expanded form, siblings or other family members can be added. Note that siblings or half siblings who were born later may not have been present at the time of a participant's particular memory. The group leader should mention that all siblings are to be included.

Participants make sketches of the family members involved and then ask themselves the question, "In what way did each individual family member mean well for the family?"

When a participant has answered the question about the positive intentions of a family member, a symbol for this intention is added to the sketch. If someone cannot find any positive intention for one or more family members, this says something about his relationship to that person, not about the other person's character. It may be an indication of a serious entanglement.

In the next phase of the exercise, each participant lays out the sketches of family members in a way that seems right. At an appropriate distance, the participant takes the meta-position and checks to see that all the sketches are placed correctly. The psycho-aesthetic element is important here. There is a very clear sense of whether a sketch is lying in the right place, and this feeling is guided by some inner image (cf. p. 36).

By assuming the position of each individual family member and then changing to the meta-position, the participants experience differences in the way relationships in the family are seen from various positions and, optimally, gain insight and awareness. The gains from this experience can be used later, depending on the focus of the group work, for example, in self-development groups, group therapy, or adult education courses. If the exercise is brought into a family constellation seminar, please bear in mind that the aim of the exercise is not to find a resolution of entanglements, which are sometimes not even apparent in this process, but rather, to facilitate awareness about relationships in the family (cf. p. 86, p. 90).

This kind of self-exploration takes place on the biographical level. In a follow-up family constellation using representatives, the entanglements become more visible and any resolution arises from the "in-forming" field, that field that contains, shapes, and informs the family. (Albrecht Mahr).

Working with the family picture, as described above, is an exercise that is applicable at the beginning of a group, but could also be introduced into an on-going process.

Description of Procedures: Basic Structure of the Family Image in a Group Setting

Prepared material: Every participant has a piece of cardboard, or something which can be using as a supporting surface for drawing, four sheets of white typing paper (A4), and three coloured pencils, pens, or chalks. The participants sit in their usual places and the group leader conducts the entire group with the following instructions. (Emphasized words are printed in italics.)

1. Position yourself so that you are *sitting comfortably* and your feet are *resting* firmly on the floor. *Leave behind you* everything you have experienced today and *let go* of any thoughts going through your mind. *Exhale deeply* ... you can feel how this deep flow of your breath takes away anything you no longer need. Slowly close your eyes and turn your attention inwards. Move your awareness down into your feet ... feel how they *rest on, and are carried by, and held by* the earth. Move your attention up and feel how your chair *carries and holds* you ... As you notice your muscles *relaxing*, you can *let go* of things that have become *unnecessary* ... As your breath gently comes in and goes out, *all by itself,* with each breath go further back into your past ... and just as the floor under you *carries* your weight, so have we all, at some time in our lives, *been carried.* Every one of us, without exception ... when we were in our mother's womb ... and so, just as we each have a mother, we each also have a father, every one of us, without exception, regardless of how life has gone on for us ... *let yourself be carried along* ... until you can see your family, the family you come from: Father, mother, and child. How old are you? ... look around - who was in the family at that time? Who had, perhaps, already died? Look at yourself as a child at that time, whether it's a memory or like a photo. When you have the feeling that these three people are alive, then take your time and slowly open your eyes when you are ready, and put your inner picture on paper.

2. With your non-dominant hand, draw a sketch of your mother, your father, and you, on three separate pieces of paper. Feel free to express these people however you wish, a realistic or abstract picture, or perhaps a symbol.

3. When you have finished, lay your papers out on the floor so that you can see all three.

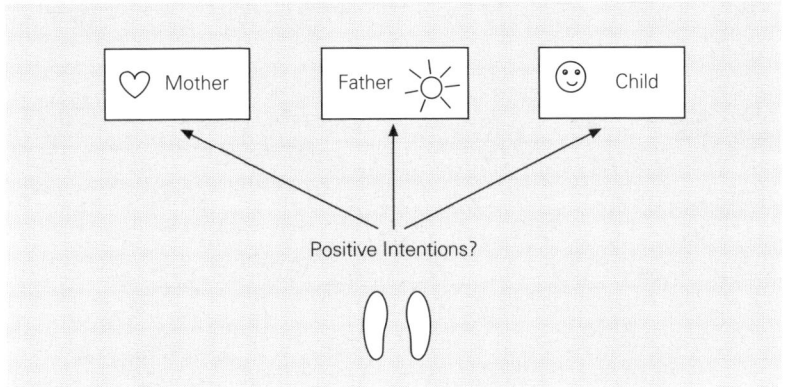

4. Imagine that you are looking through the eyes of each individual person and ask yourself the following questions:
   – How did each individual in your family mean well?
   – What good intentions did they have for the family?
   – How was the love of your mother and father expressed so that it allowed you to grow up?

Make a small symbol that expresses the good intentions of that person on each paper. Think about which direction the person is looking in, and draw a small arrow to indicate that direction.

5. Arrange yourselves in the room so that you each have enough space around you. Lay your papers on the floor in a way that corresponds to your inner picture of your family. Pay attention to the way each person is looking, the angles, and distance from each other. Make sure your papers are far enough away from your neighbour's papers. Put the blank piece of paper at an adequate distance (meta-position) and stand on this paper. How do you experience your family from this position? Can you see the positive intentions of the individual family members?

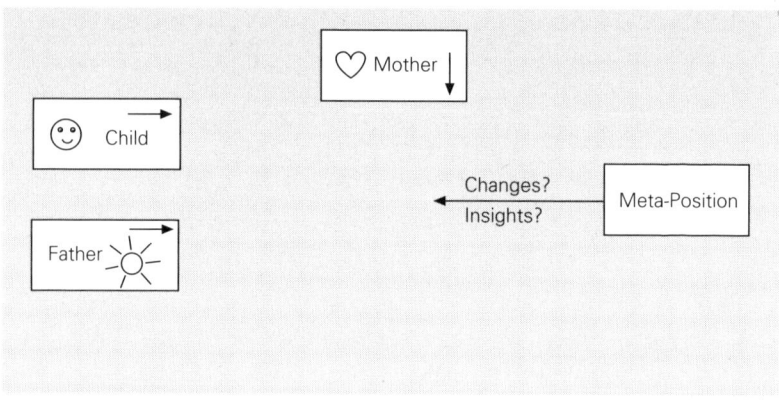

6. Stand in the position of your father and pay attention to your physical and emotional reactions. How are you standing? How are you breathing? What do you notice? How does it feel for the father to stand in this family? How is his love for his wife and child expressed?

7. Move to the meta-position and look at your family from the outside again. Has anything changed through your standing in your father's position?

8. Stand in the position of your mother and notice your physical and emotional reactions. How do you feel as the mother in this family? How do you perceive the relationship between your husband and your child? In what way have you, as mother, intended something good for the family? How is your love expressed?

9. Return to the meta-position. Has anything changed in your awareness of the whole?

10. Stand in the position of the child at that time and notice your physical and emotional reactions again. What is the relationship like with your father and with your mother? When you look at your parents, do you feel larger, smaller, or the same? How did you, as a child, intend something good for your family? How was your love expressed?

11. Return to the meta-position and look at the whole picture once again. What has changed? Do you have any insights or new understanding?

12. Return to your original place with your papers and share your experiences.

Extended Family Image

If space and time allow, the family image can be extended to include others in the core family. Those who belong to the family of origin are, for example, all the siblings, living and dead. These are also sketched on separate pieces of paper and treated in the same way described above.

Depending on the focus and aim of the group, the exercise can naturally be expanded to include grandparents. The principle remains the same: Looking at relationships in light of the positive intentions of those involved.

In a further variation of the family image, the female participants make and lay out sketches of the line of the female side of their family: Mother, grandmother, great-grandmother, etc. The men in the group do the same thing with the male line in their family. The line of ancestors of the same gender (Baxa, Essen, and Essen 1999) can be a powerful resource for strength.

NIG in Supervision

The representation of a relationship network through sketches or symbols may be a valuable tool for supervision. The person being supervised, for example, can lay out his image of a client's family of origin in relation to himself. The institution the therapist works for, an insurance company that provides payment, etc, could also be represented. By looking through the eyes of various parts of the system and using feedback from the supervisor, the therapist can find a good place for himself within the network. This also often gives some indication if and how the client's relationship system is being seen and acknowledged.

If the person in supervision is trying to decide whether or not to continue working with a particular client, the exercise of "two sides" is useful. There is one side that wants to continue the work, and another side that has the feeling that it is not, or is no longer functional.

In this case, the therapist might draw a sketch of how he sees his client, another sketch of how he thinks his client sees him, and a third representing how he thinks the supervisor sees him and his client in these representations. The sketches are laid out in the room together with a blank page for the meta-position. The supervisor can wait to see which NIG element develops during the movements back and forth between the positions. Experience has shown that a relevant whole usually emerges on its own and provides new directions for the work. The essential qualities in this exercise are remaining calm and collected, and leaving enough room for the autonomy of the unconscious, "the inner artist". In addition, one should be aware that the results of such a process make a statement primarily about the relationship between the therapist and his client. Whether the client's entanglements can be seen in this way is questionable, although it is very likely that there will be indications of where to look for a solution. Still, in the next session with the client, the therapist should handle this kind of information very cautiously and look carefully at the measure of truth.

8. Extending Applications to Other Methods

THE PRACTICE OF INTEGRATION

The subtitle of this book is *"The Creative Use of Constellations ..."*. In the chapter describing the various procedures, we have already mentioned the fact that as a practitioner gains experience with the NIG elements, the potential for creative use of the elements increases. The same is true of combining Neuro-Imaginative Gestalting with other methods. Each of you will notice, perhaps even while reading, what might be suitable in your own practice. You can complement NIG with elements of methods you already use, or integrate elements of NIG into your own preferred methods. In this way you will find and shape your own personal style of using Neuro-Imaginative Gestalting. For example, individual sketches from NIG exercises could be taken for use in art therapy for working "on the picture" (cf. p. 24). In the context of body therapy, a particular posture (e. g. "looking down from above") or a particular movement (e. g. bowing down) can be looked at more intensively. Another example might be muscle tension connected to the dynamics of an entanglement, which could be relieved by additional massage or bio-energetic exercises. NIG elements such as the "two sides" or the "family image" can be complemented and expanded by various techniques used in mediating marital conflict.

NIG AS A WAY OF INTEGRATING FAMILY CONSTELLATION WITH OTHER METHODS

Colleagues from a variety of backgrounds wish to integrate the family constellations developed by Bert Hellinger, or the knowledge gained from this approach, in the methods they already use. The NIG elements of the family image and family constellations can be used without other NIG elements.

125

NIG as a Complement to Family Constellations

Other therapists have made family constellations the focus of their work and may be interested in complementary approaches for individual work. The elements of NIG are particularly suitable for this, as this approach has been developed exactly for that reason. Nonetheless, the therapist's repertoire should be broader, since NIG is not a self-contained method of therapy (cf. p. 14).

Example Kinesiology

As an example of a complementary application of NIG with another method, the following section describes in more detail how Neuro-Imaginative Gestalting and Kinesiology work together in practice, resulting in benefits for both approaches.

In the introduction to this book, we have encouraged you, dear reader, to participate in the creation of the book by choosing the chapters that appeal to you the most. Those of you who are not familiar with kinesiology are free to skip over the next section, or read on if your curiosity has been aroused.

Short Introduction to Kinesiology

The first problem with talking about kinesiology is that within this area, there are a great many forms, ranging from medical/dental, educational, and psychotherapeutic, to the realms of music and sport. What all of these have in common is that they are rooted in Traditional Chinese Medicine (TCM), and come from the "Applied Kinesiology" developed by the American doctor George Goodheart, beginning in 1960. Applied Kinesiology is a synthesis of Chinese and western medicine. The main tool is the muscle test, which serves to identify and localize disruptive factors in the body. The basic principles of Applied Kinesiology have been developed in countless directions and into other areas of specialization. Here, primarily the following kinesiological methods have been taken into account (Innecken 2000).

– *Touch for Health* according to Dr. John F. Thie (holistic medicine, preventative medicine)

- *Edu-Kinesthetic, Brain Gym* according to Dr. Paul and Gail Dennison (education, special education)
- *Three in One Concepts (3 in 1)* according to Gordon Stokes, Daviel Whiteside, and Candace Callaway (psychology)
- *Psycho-Kinesiology* according to Dr. Dietrich Klinghardt (holistic medicine, systemic orientated psychotherapy).

Psycho-Kinesiology is particularly suitable as a complement to family constellations and NIG, since with this method, you can discover and work with unresolved inner conflicts that come from the personal history or from a systemic entanglement. The other kinesiological methods above, which share much in common with NLP structures, can also be easily integrated with NIG elements.

In all the methods of kinesiology mentioned, the muscle test serves as a bio-feedback process that can identify physical, psychological, and mental disturbances. Disruptive factors might include, for example, dental problems, scar tissue disruptions, food allergies, heavy metal contamination, or even unresolved emotional conflicts. If the muscle test pinpoints one or more of these disruptions as a cause of symptoms or problems, the next step is to find an appropriate treatment for this problem in the present. The muscle test is again useful for this purpose.

A Model of the Five Levels of Healing

As Dietrich Klinghardt has depicted in his model of the five levels of healing (Klinghardt 1996), problems or symptoms arise on different levels, from the physical to the spiritual, and can also be treated on different levels.

The Five "Bodies" of the Human Being	Examples of Treatment
5ᵗʰ Level Spiritual Body	Prayer Self-Healing
4ᵗʰ Level Intuitive Body	Family Constellations Jungian Psychotherapy
3ʳᵈ Level Mental Body	Homeopathy Psychotherapy
2ⁿᵈ Level Electro-Magnetic Body	Acupuncture Body Work
1ˢᵗ Level Physical Body	Medicine Physical Therapy

In this model, Klinghardt assumes that problems or symptoms should be treated at the level where they arise. An accident injury, for example, would naturally be treated at the level of the physical body (level 1). In addition, Klinghardt assumes that therapeutic intervention at a higher level, quickly has a strong effect on lower levels, whereas the lower levels work more slowly and less effectively on higher levels. With the example of the accident injury, one could treat the traumatic aspect of the accident with psychotherapy or also kinesiology methods (level 3), and thereby contribute to a faster healing of the injury. If one looks at the accident in the context of the family system, for example, in a constellation (level 4), patterns might be detected that indicate repetitions over several generations. Such work on the fourth level, the level of archaic orders, may have a powerful effect on the physical body, but Bert Hellinger himself has emphasized the necessity of also coordinating other, primarily medical, procedures (Hellinger 2001).

To do justice to each client individually, we strongly advise that various specialist approaches and therapeutic methods be considered. Kinesiology is also useful here in that the muscle test locates the causative factors of the problem and makes clear which level of treatment is appropriate.

Reciprocal Effects of Kinesiology and NIG

Regardless of whether one is working at the third level, which is primarily biographical, or at the fourth level, which focuses on the archaic orders of relationships, experience has proven that Neuro-Imaginative Gestalting and the various methods of kinesiology complement each other and have beneficial reciprocal effects. Since the structure of this book is limited, we will examine only one of the possible ways of combining NIG and kinesiology, to the enrichment of both. In terms of time, this combination can be used within one therapy session or at various points in the whole therapeutic process.

Practical Example of the Complementary Use of NIG and Kinesiology

"Blocked Regulation"

In Psycho-Kinesiology, according to Klinghardt, the autonomic nervous system is tested at the beginning of every session. One can speak of an open, or of a blocked regulation. The autonomic nervous system may be blocked or limited by factors at various levels according to the model presented above. As previously stated, the disruptive factors could include scars, teeth, heavy metal contamination, geopathic stress factors, food incompatibilities, or unresolved psychological conflicts. By working through the disruptive factors on the various levels of the model presented, the autonomic nervous system can become functional again, and a client is more likely to be ready and able to open up and overcome old patterns.

Example: Ten-year-old Maximilian has suffered for years from headaches and nausea, but no physical cause has been determined. The kinesiological test results show a "blocked regulation", caused by scar tissue disturbance. The boy had a number of heart operations as an infant and carries scars on his chest. Treatment to relieve the disruptive effects of the scars brings about an open regulation and improvement in the symptoms. In the following kinesiological session, the trauma from the operations is treated by tapping on certain acupuncture points in the meridian system. The symptoms are again significantly relieved but have not completely disappeared. In the next session, a muscle test indicates a systemic entanglement. Maximilian's mother is questioned and reports that her brother died at an early age. As she relates this fact, Maximilian bursts into tears. The therapist asks him to draw two sketches, one of himself and one of this uncle that he has never met. As he lays out the sketches and enters into these images, it becomes clear that the child tends to carry the suffering of his uncle and to follow him. Maximilian moves back and forth between the two sketches a number of times. From the meta-position, he determines that his uncle hopes with all his heart that things go well for his nephew. Finally, the therapist has him stand on his own sketch and say to his uncle, "Dear Uncle, you have a place in my heart forever. I leave you with the burden." After this session, the boy's headaches and nausea disappear within the next weeks.

Neurogenic Switching

In addition to "regulation", the integration of the two halves of the brain is tested in each kinesiology session. A disrupted connection between the hemispheres is described as "neurogenic switching". This "switching" is also caused by factors on the various levels according to the model, factors which can be tested using kinesiology. The right and left half of the brain have very different tasks in the life of a human being. A simplified description would be analytical and holistic orientations. A disruption in the integration of these two sides has an effect on the mind, body, and soul. For example, it limits movement and thought patterns and also the development of personality (Innecken 2000). A therapist working with kinesiology can eliminate the "neurogenic switching" and thereafter turn to the work with NIG. This process has proven useful as a neurological preparation for the work with NIG, particularly, of course, the "two sides" exercise. An example of how the work with "neurogenic switching" can lead into an NIG element is detailed in the case study entitled "*Line of Resolutions: Or Everyone Belongs*" (cf. p. 163).

Another example of complementary work with NIG and kinesiology in hemispheric integration: The client imagines her right brain and her left brain and makes a sketch representing each on separate pieces of paper. She stands on each sketch in turn, noticing the qualities of each. After the kinesiology integration work, which, for example, might consist of a combination of particular eye movements and body movements, she stands on each of the two sketches again. The surprise at the change in perceptions is usually marked, and is an experience children, in particular, very much enjoy.

Goals

Working on goals is of particular value in kinesiology. Goals are formulated verbally and very precisely according to the criteria of "appropriate goals". Taking into consideration the aspect of a vague concept of goals (cf. p. 33), which children can accomodate, the client can be asked to make a sketch of the current problem and a sketch of the state of having reached the goal and then to stand in each position. The client pays attention to his physical and emotional reactions and, following the kinesiology work, returns to the two positions again. Again, it is surprising to see the changes in perception that occur.

Family Image

The NIG exercise with the family image can be included at various points in kinesiology work. For example, it could be a support at the beginning of a session, while talking about the problem. If, for example, the client is having difficulty seeing her own participation in a problem ("my mother just won't let go of me, I always have to be there for her"), she might stand first on a sketch of her mother and then on a sketch of herself. The insight that emerges from this change of perspective determines the direction to go next.

The family image is also appropriate for use in the search for resources at the beginning of a session. ("Who would be most likely to have confidence that you will improve in school?") At the end of the session the client can stand in the position of the resource person and notice any changes (cf. p. 52).

Working with Trauma

If a trauma is activated or strong emotions aroused in the course of an NIG exercise such as re-imprinting, you can work with this using the kinesiological methods from trauma therapy, such as EMDR (Eye Movement Desensitization Reprocessing) from Shapiro, Klinghardt's work with coloured glasses, eye movements, or the tapping acupressure method used by Callahan and others.

Working with Belief Systems

Traumatic events in a person's life or in the family are stored in the unconscious in the form of beliefs that may have a limiting effect ("I am not worthy of this life" or "Whenever things are going well for me, something bad happens"). These "beliefs" have a powerful influence on behaviour and health (cf. p. 55). If we can locate the source of the limiting beliefs by using the muscle test, and work with them, they can be replaced by liberating beliefs. (For example, "I am valuable," or "It's all right if things go well for me.") At the end of a kinesiology session, a good addition might be to sketch the newly discovered belief and stand in that position. This provides an experience that goes beyond what would be possible with language alone.

Family Constellations

As previously mentioned, indications may arise in Psycho-Kinesiology that point to a systemic entanglement, in the sense of Hellinger's work. If such a dynamic appears in the course of the work, a therapist who is competent in constellation work can do a family constellation with sketches or symbols at this point, as described in the descriptions of the NIG elements. In this process, the relationship to another member of the family becomes visible and can be felt. In optimal cases, a resolution can be found by adding other persons, changing the positions of the spatial anchors, or by using resolving sentences or rituals.

An example: During her summer holidays, Ms Beckmann suffers an inexplicable panic attack while swimming. Using the kinesiological method of muscle testing, it becomes clear that there is a connection to a dramatic event in her family. Her mother's brother drowned at the age of two. The therapist asks Ms Beckmann to lay out a symbol for herself and one for her uncle. As she stands on her own position facing her uncle, she is seized by an overwhelming grief over his death. With the words, "I would have so liked to have known you. I now give you a place in my heart", she feels great love for him. At the therapist's suggestion she says, "In my love for you, I feel like you." Ms Beckmann nods her agreement with this sentence. After having changed places back and forth several times and bowing to her uncle and his fate, Ms Beckmann can say to him, "I honour and respect your fate and I leave it with you." She then feels calm and clear. After such a constellation you could conclude the session with integrative kinesiology work. In this particular case, the therapist chose not to do any additional work.

9. Case Examples

CASE EXAMPLES: BARBARA INNECKEN

The following case studies from therapeutic practice show diverse possibilities for working creatively with Neuro-Imaginative Gestalting.

The first four case descriptions proceed similarly to the descriptions of procedure in chapter six. They include the use of the meta-position, interrupting patterns, the life path, and the exercise with two sides.

The case involving the positive intentions of symptoms shows how a portion of an NIG element can be used as a special focus point. In addition, this example contains a variation of NIG using abstract symbols (round and rectangular felt pieces) instead of sketches as spatial anchors. The following session, which is also documented here, is a good example of a family constellation in individual work.

The case dealing with the two sides, "solitude and solidarity", exemplifies the way group representatives can be used in NIG exercises. In this case the two sides, or inner characteristics, are represented by group members and related to events in the client's family.

The last case, "the line of resolutions, everyone belongs", makes clear that the NIG structures described in this book are intended as a stimulus. When a therapist reacts creatively and flexibly to the individual personality and situation of a client, something new and unique may develop.

With the exception of the case of the constellation of two sides, all the case study descriptions include the initial situation, the issue at hand, and the procedure followed, as well as the effects of the work and their place in the therapeutic process.

Names and details have been changed to protect the anonymity of the people involved.

THE META-POSITION: ADVICE OF THE WISE WOMAN

Initial Situation/Problem

Mrs Miller, 37 years old, is married with two children. She would like to move out of the flat she shares with her husband. "I feel like I can't breathe. My husband's parents live in the same house. Maybe it's because of them. My husband is away at work a lot. We have grown apart and hardly talk to each other." Her husband does not want her to move out, and is less dissatisfied with the current situation than she is.

Issue

Mrs Miller wants to find out if moving out is the right thing to do. At the moment it seems to be the only way open to her that would allow her to be herself. At the same time, she is afraid that the relationship with her husband will completely disintegrate, which is not what she wants at this point in time.

Procedure

The therapist asks the client to sketch the current situation with her husband. Using a black pencil, Mrs Miller portrays herself and her husband in profile. Her husband is looking at her from behind, whereas she is looking forward, away from him.

Present

As Mrs Miller stands on the sketch of her present situation, she experiences pressure in her chest that makes breathing difficult. She is also aware of a very uncomfortable shivering down her back. "My husband is looking at me from behind. I don't like that at all!"

134

The therapist asks if things have always been like this in their relationship, or if there was a time when things were better. Mrs Miller nods and her face lights up. "Oh yes, the beginning of our relationship, before we had children and before we lived with his parents, that was totally different. We were a happy young couple!" As a symbol of this happy time, Mrs Miller sketches a river. Above the river, her relationship flows in a parallel way in red and yellow. She is asked to visualize her marriage in the present and the past on a time line. On the floor, she lays out the picture of the past rather distant from the picture of the present.

Present

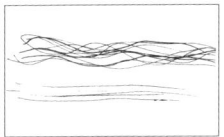

Past

As Mrs Miller stands in the position of the past, she spreads her arms and exclaims, "It feels so bright and flowing!"

In view of these seemingly irreconcilable feelings, the therapist asks, "Imagine you could see into the future. What would be a good resolution for you?" The client looks at the sketches of the qualities of the present and the past relationship thoughtfully again, and then draws a sketch of a yellow laughing sun, containing two people in profile, looking at each other. She places this paper relatively close to the picture of the present.

Good Solution

Meta-Position

Present

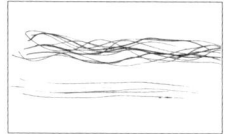

Past

As the client stands on the picture of a good solution, she straightens up and her voice becomes firm and serious. "Yes, that would be a good solution. The two are looking at each other and going on their way together."

The therapist asks Mrs Miller to lay out a blank piece of paper in a place where she can look at the configuration of the timeline from the outside (meta-position). "This is the place of the wise woman. She knows life, she knows about men and women. How does she see the relationship of these two people?" In saying this, the therapist introduces the concept of a change of perspective, which Mrs Miller is happy to try out.

From the meta-position, in the role of the wise woman, the situation is clear and distinct: An abbreviated version of this couple's story is lying in front of her. They want to get back together. They want to deal with each other. They began in red and yellow harmony, are now in a crisis, portrayed in black, and they are prepared to meet each other as mature adults in the future, in which the colours of red and yellow are the same as the colours used for the beginning of their relationship. Asked whether, in the role of the wise woman, she has any advice that would lead out of the crisis to a good solution, Mrs Miller suggests the following:

- The woman should give herself and her husband some time.
- She should pay more attention to herself, instead of looking at her husband's family. Then she would have more strength for herself, and it would also be good for her husband.

The client finds the wise woman's advice a clear and helpful answer to her problem. The therapy session is finished.

Effects

Mrs Miller comes for another session five weeks later. She reports that she has followed the wise woman's advice and the relationship with her husband is much better. She is not considering moving out at the moment. In paying more attention to herself, however, she has become aware of fears that are now problematic for her. Working with psycho-kinesiology, a connection shows up between her fears and her father's suicide. The work on this includes kinesiology and spatial anchors. The fears resolve slowly after this work. A few months later the couple do a family constellation in a group. It shows that Mrs Miller cannot look at her husband as she only has eyes for her dead brother. When she has grieved for her brother, weeping copiously, she looks at her husband with love. Mr M also has to re-solve an identification with his mother's first love before he is able to take his wife in his arms happily.

INTERRUPTING PATTERNS: THE RUCKSACKS

Preface

There are many ways to alter the pattern of the complaint, as de Shazer calls it. In the case at hand, the interruption of the pattern begins with the first question following the initial interview. "Are there times or situations in your life when you experience your son differently?" (de Shazer 1988). The client then looks at this exception to the pattern. She makes a sketch, places it in the room, and notices the effects in her physical reactions. The experience confirms her present view of the problem. The therapists supports her efforts in looking for a solution with circular questions, "How does your son experience these exceptions?" The change of perspective includes her son's experience rather than just her own. This permits the client to look at the problems up to now in a different way. The interruption of the previous pattern causes a certain amount of confusion, which is organized and resolved finally from the dissociated position of the neutral observer.

As described in chapter four in the section "through the eyes of another" (cf. p. 51), looking at a problem from various perspectives may have therapeutic value for a client and can even lead to resolution. In this case, the mother is relieved that her son likes to carry his little rucksack and is setting out on his way with a feeling of being supported. She and her son both accept the path the family seems to be heading along together.

Three months later, a family constellation reveals an unexpected connection at the deeper level of the systemic orders of relationships. The client integrates and works through this in a kind of inner family constellation a year later.

Initial Situation/Problem

Mrs Kern, 42 years old, is married and is very concerned about her eleven-year-old son, who suffers from migraines. She feels partially responsible for his headaches, since she suffered the same thing as a child, and now feels that she has passed on the suffering. Mrs Kern's family on her mother's side were persecuted in the Third Reich. Mrs Kern has worked on this topic many times using kinesiology and family constellations. Now, however, she is afraid that the fate of her family of origin is having an effect on her son, and she is worried that she is not strong enough as a mother.

Issue

Mrs Kern wants to be able to support her son without burdening him with her own fears.

Procedure

The therapist asks the client to make a sketch of the problem as she sees it. In the drawing, which is done completely in blue, a bowed down woman is leaning on her walking stick. Her son stands opposite her. Since Mrs Kern is very moved and weeping as she draws the sketch, the therapist asks her about any exceptions to the problem. "Are there, or have there been any times or situations in your life, when you were able to be with your son in a different way, not so heavily weighed down by problems?"

Mrs Kern stops and draws herself, looking happy with her arms around her son. She chooses red pastel chalk for this picture. She lays both papers on the floor.

Problem

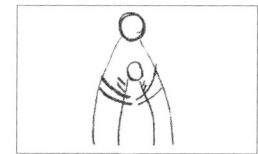
Exception to the Problem

As the client stands on her sketches, in the position of the problem she feels predictably burdened and has difficulty standing up. In the position of the exception to the problem, however, she gets a surprise. The exception to the problem does not feel centred and protective, as she had imagined, but rather cramped and oppressive. Through this unexpected experience, Mrs Kern sees her negative view of herself as a mother confirmed. "No matter what I do, it's always bad for my son!"

The therapist decides to move to a change of perspective through circular questioning. "How do you think your son felt at the times when you held him in your arms like in your drawing?" Mrs Kern is visibly happy to take up this question and answers the question with a sketch of a shallow bowl, completely in red (exception to the problem from the son's viewpoint).

Exception to the Problem
from Son's Viewpoint

Problem from
Client's Viewpoint

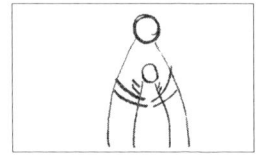

Exception to the Problem
from Client's Viewpoint

When the client stands on this sketch, she feels a pleasant warmth through her whole body, but also feels closed in. She wishes there were more space to move. Despite the feeling of being crowded, Mrs Kern stands noticeably straighter and her facial expression is more relaxed.

As it is clearly helpful for the client to look at her problem from a different perspective, the therapist says, "Earlier you drew a picture of the problem from your viewpoint. How do you think this situation would look from your son's viewpoint?"

Her face exhibits surprise at the question, but she draws the next sketch without hesitation (problem from the son's viewpoint). All in blue, she draws herself and her son walking along a path, each carrying a rucksack.

Problem from Son's
Viewpoint

Exception to the Problem
from Son's Viewpoint

Problem from
Client's Viewpoint

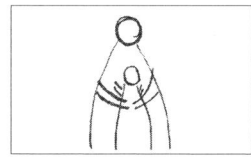

Exception to the Problem
from Client's Viewpoint

When Mrs Kern stands in the position of the problem from her son's point of view, the process takes an amazing turn. She feels light in this position, nods a few times in agreement, and says, "Yes. This is good. Now I have enough room and I also feel like setting off. My back is warm and I have a good companion!" This extremely positive reaction to the problem from her son's viewpoint clearly confuses Mrs Kern.

To give her an opportunity to think about her impressions, the therapist asks her to look at the whole thing again from the outside, from the position of the neutral observer. A blank piece of paper is used to mark the meta-position.

Problem from Son's
Viewpoint

Exception to the Problem
from Son's Viewpoint

Problem from Client's
Viewpoint

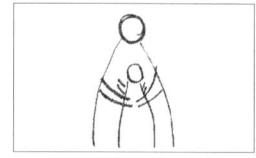

Exception to the Problem
from Client's Viewpoint

Meta-Position

As Mrs Kern stands in the position of a neutral observer, the problem from the son's viewpoint is clearly the solution. The client's old pattern of burdened mother with a cane is not tenable in view of her reaction from the son's perspective. As a neutral observer Mrs Kern states, "Mother and son are both satisfied and they accept their situation as it is. They are going together along a common path, but clearly separately. Each carries a rucksack that is the right size for them. Where is the problem?"

Effects

With this therapy session, Mrs Kern felt a marked lessening of her fears.

After about three months, she and her husband come to do a family constellation because her son's health has worsened. In the constellation, the symptom appears in a completely new connection. Mrs Kern's father had an uncle who killed himself at the end of the Second World War. The only thing that is known about him was that he was a fervent Nazi. In the constellation it is clear how strongly the fate and the deeds of this uncle have affected the family, particularly Mrs Kern and her son. It is clearly important for Mrs Kern, both for herself and for her son, to look at the perpetrator's acts in her family, since she has previously only looked at the victim side of her family, on her mother's side.

After about a year, Mrs Kern reports that her son's migraines seldom occur, and are also much milder. She has had a very special experience. In a kind of inner film-like fantasy, she imagined asking her son for his rucksack. As she noticed that carrying her own rucksack and that of her son was beyond her strength, she decided to lay both rucksacks at her father's feet. She did this with a feeling of great excitement and then she bowed down for a long time. Since then she has felt relieved in a very unique way and can confidently watch her son growing up.

THE LIFE PATH: ALL A CHILD NEEDS IS LOVE

As mentioned, work with the life path can be useful in various phases of development, for example, in an acute crisis it can be used to direct attention towards solutions and away from the problem; or, following a phase of therapy in which a lot of clearing out of past issues has been possible, it may serve to develop new strength by looking forwards. In the case at hand, the situation is more a pause along the life path after a difficult passage in the past, to find strength and space for new directions.

Initial Situation/Problem

Mrs Gruber is a fifty-six-year-old business woman. She is married and has a twenty-year-old daughter. Her husband had a serious accident a few years ago and since then has suffered from physical and psychological problems. His condition has improved recently. Mrs Gruber is noticing now, for the first time, how much she has been looking at her husband and the good of the family and how little attention she has paid to her own inner well-being. She believes, however, that it has always been easier for her to worry about others than about herself. Mrs Gruber has previously had a client-centred therapy and has done family constellations.

Issue

Mrs Gruber would like to become more aware of herself and her needs and pay more attention to these aspects of her life.

Procedure

The therapist asks Mrs Gruber to use her non-dominant hand to sketch her current problem and her concept of the goal. She is asked to lay out these sketches on the floor and add a blank paper to mark the meta-position, in this case a wise old woman who knows about life and people.

Concept of Goal

Meta-Position

Problem in Present

In the drawing of the problem in the present there is a meadow. Mrs Gruber comments, "Something's missing, but all around there is a lot of space. It is open." She stands on this sketch and feels a pleasant pulsating in her chest, and feels drawn inwards. She has a sense of being well-anchored up as far as her knees, and is swaying a bit above that level. As she looks at the goal, she exhales in relief. She moves to stand on the goal sketch, a radiant heart, and closes her eyes. Her breathing deepens. Her feet are still planted firmly, but her body is still swaying from the knees up. As she stands in the meta-position, in the role of the wise old woman, she realizes, "I think the distance to the goal is much shorter than Mrs Gruber thinks. I think she has great potential!"

The therapist asks Mrs Gruber if she can remember any steps she has taken in the past that allowed her to take good care of herself. Mrs Gruber nods in a cheerful way and sketches the following positive steps and decisions in her life up until now: Resource 1 is her decision to go to a particular school, where she felt comfortable. Resource 2 is the decision to get her driving license, despite her foster mother's fears. Resource 3 is the marriage to her husband. Resource 4 is her decision to have a child even though for many years of her married life she did not want children. Resource 5 represents her professional training. Resource 6 is her decision to go on a trip alone when her intended travelling companions had to cancel on short notice. She had never done this before.

Concept of Goal

Meta-Position

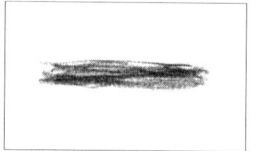

Problem in Present

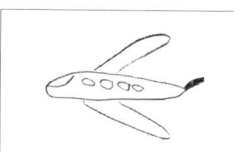

Resource 6

Resource 4

Resource 5

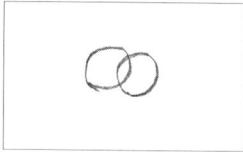

Resource 3

Resource 2

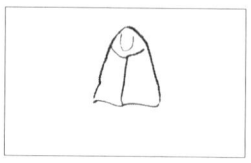

Resource 1

Even while she is still in the process of drawing and explaining resources 1 (school choice) and resource 4 (decision to have a child), Mrs Gruber is already very touched and in tears. She is asked to look at her life path from the perspective of the wise woman. In this position, her reaction is similar. When she looks at her decision to have a child she bursts into tears. The therapist asks her to test out how far away the meta-position has to be to allow her, in her role of the wise woman, to look at this event calmly. A good place is found and the wise woman concludes that when Mrs Gruber decided to have a child and became pregnant, she was very afraid that she would not be a good mother to this child because her own mother died shortly after Mrs Gruber was born. The therapist asks how the situation turned out when the child was actually there. The wise woman answers, "Mrs Gruber was often unsure of herself with her daughter, but she has always loved her child. That is all a child needs!"

Strengthened by this observation, Mrs Gruber is able to stand in the position of each resource and feel their positive effects on her physically and emotionally. To fill out this feeling, the therapist asks Mrs Gruber if there is a person in her past or present who would have faith in her ability to reach her goal. Mrs Gruber looks radiant. "Yes, there is! That is my teacher, who I have been learning from for almost twenty years!" She lays a paper for the resource person not, as might be expected, in the past, but next to the goal. She stands in this position and is confirmed in her belief about her teacher's good opinion of her.

Mrs Gruber returns to the past once more, collects all her resources, and lays the whole stack under the sketch of the problem in the present. When she stands on this "cushioned" present, she exhales audibly and feels a pulsing red-orange strength in her body. "The path to the goal seems much shorter to me now," she says in surprise, and, carrying her papers with her, she moves closer to the goal position until it feels like a good distance.

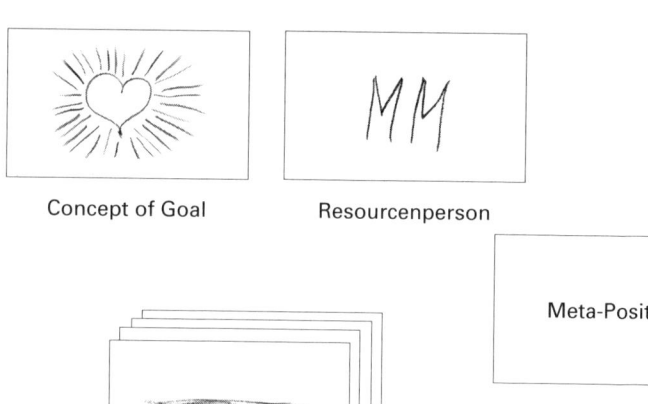

Concept of Goal　　Resourcenperson

Meta-Position

Problem in Present

Next, Mrs Gruber takes her resource sketches with her as she moves to the concept of the goal. "This is a piece of cake!", she laughs as she stands in the position of the goal concept and looks back at the distance from the present. In this position she feels similar to the way she felt at the beginning, but the feeling is more intense: A pleasant pulsation in her chest and a feeling of being drawn inwards. The therapist asks Mrs Gruber if, looking from this position, she can identify any concrete steps that are useful on the way to the goal. "A good next step would be to look more closely at the fear of failure I felt back then as a young mother."

When Mrs Gruber takes the position of the teacher, the concrete steps are expressed as, "You don't have to do anything. Stay clearly in the here and now. That's enough."

Finally, Mrs Gruber stands in the position of the wise woman and her advice is, "Be patient and stay on your path!"

Effects

After about three months, Mrs Gruber reports that she stands on her sketches every so often and when she does, she feels light and soft. She increasingly has the feeling that her husband is a support, instead of the feeling she is dragging him along. She now feels like she has permission to worry about her own needs. In the near future she would like to look at what is "hers" more carefully, in a therapeutic setting.

Two Sides: Something is Still Missing Here!

Preface

When a client experiences ambivalence regarding a particular topic, the task is always one of communication with these two sides that appear irreconcilable. It is not important whether these two sides are inner parts of the person or whether they are influences from other people. What is essential is that both parts get to have their say and that both are honoured.

In this case example, a resolution of the inner conflict is sought using various aspects of the procedures for "two sides" described on page 106. As often happens when using NIG, solutions emerge in the therapeutic process out of an interplay between various basic elements.

The first thing that is immediately apparent is that the client draws only half a sketch for each of the two opposing parts. By opening up the space of resolution, the client, from the meta-position, recognizes the opportunity for integrating the two sides. However, before the solution can become clear, agreement is needed from the parts or persons who have not participated. In this case, it is the client's children. Although the resolution, an alternative for action in the future, is considered to be a good one by all those involved, the neutral observer advises that the polarity be left for a while longer to allow time for the solution to be realised.

Initial Situation/Problem

Mrs Reichelt, forty-nine years old, was divorced two years ago. She has got two adult children. The decision to get a divorce was not easy, and she came to that decision only after years of consideration and therapeutic assistance. She has done family constellations of her present family and of her family of origin. Since separating from her husband, Mrs Reichelt has been living with a new partner. She does not see this man as the reason for her divorce. Although she is happy living with her new partner, she is still drawn to her ex-husband and feels somewhat half-hearted about the new relationship.

Issue

Mrs Reichelt would like to find a resolution of her inner split, which is causing her suffering.

Procedure

Through her previous therapeutic work, Mrs Reichelt has already looked at entanglements and solutions in her family. The therapist decides to focus the work on the two opposing sides in the client herself, the inner family.

Firstly, Mrs Reichelt is asked to draw a sketch of the two inner parts of herself, each on a separate piece of paper, and lay them out on the floor. Mrs Reichelt draws half of a broken heart representing her desire to return to her ex-husband (Return to Husband 1) and half of a sun for the warmth and security she experiences with her new partner (Relationship with Partner 2).

Return to Husband 1

Relationship with Partner 2

As the client stands on each of the spatial anchors, she feels even more strongly the ambivalence that is so often present in her everyday life. She feels the missing half of each picture as ice-cold and empty, and on each picture, her whole body feels drawn over to the other image. This makes her very unstable, and she can stand up straight only with difficulty.

By adding the meta-position, in this case called the neutral observer, a change of perspective is made possible. In this position, Mrs Reichelt sees that each part is missing a half, and they could possibly complement each other. Mrs Reichelt folds each paper in half and lays them close together to form a whole.

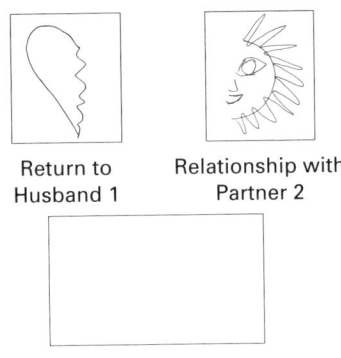

Return to Husband 1   Relationship with Partner 2

Meta-Position

When the client now stands on each inner part, her physical reaction has changed completely. She can stand on either paper with stability and feels warmth on both sides of her body. She notices, however, that she is looking into empty space and remarks, "Something is still missing here!" She goes back to the drawing table and draws two intersecting circles on a piece of paper. Looking closer, she shakes her head and puts the paper aside, saying, "That's not right!"

She makes a second sketch of two circles that are not touching, which matches her image. "These are my children," she says, and lays the paper on the floor.

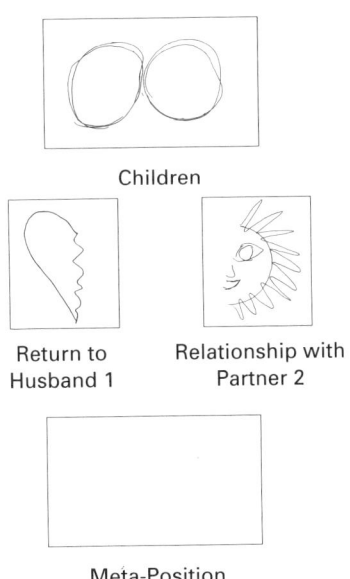

Children

Return to Husband 1   Relationship with Partner 2

Meta-Position

Mrs Reichelt is satisfied at first that she can see her children from either inner part, but after a short time she begins to have some doubts. "The children are important, but this isn't the right place for them." She tries out several different positions and decides on the following arrangement:

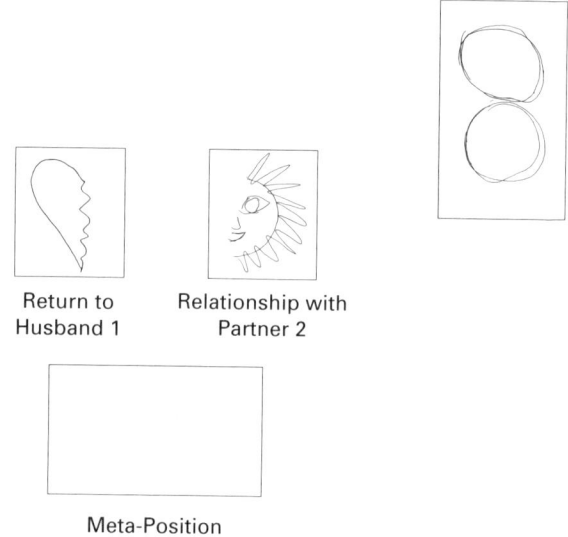

Return to
Husband 1

Relationship with
Partner 2

Meta-Position

The children have a good place now, but the problem is back that Mrs Reichelt is looking into emptiness from the position of the two inner parts. Although both parts want something to look at, Mrs Reichelt cannot decide who or what that would be. In this situation, the neutral observer is once again helpful. From the position of the observer, Mrs Reichelt looks over at the drawing table and notices the sketch with the intersecting rings that she had discarded. "This drawing was right after all. It belongs where both parts can see it!" The neutral observer can also answer the therapist's question about what it represents. "It represents marriage to the present partner."

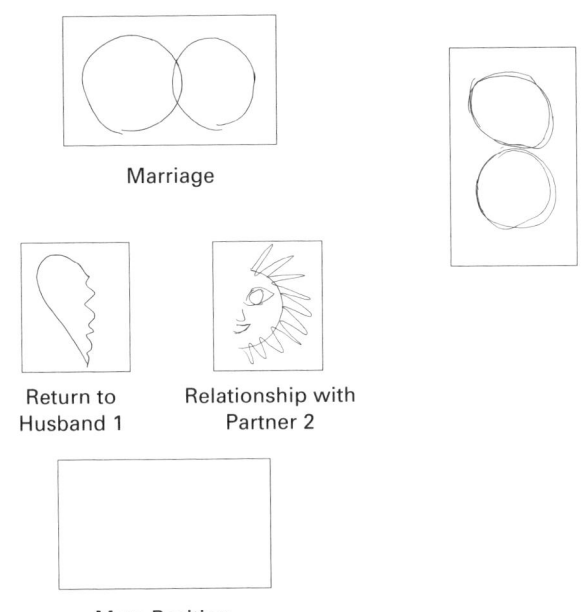

Marriage

Return to
Husband 1

Relationship with
Partner 2

Meta-Position

Mrs Reichelt stands on each spatial anchor and notices physically and emotionally that all the parts and people represented are in agreement with the solution that is now visible. The part that wanted to return to her first husband looks steadily at the marriage to the second partner, exhales in relief, and nods. The part that wants to stay in the relationship with the second partner says, "I have wanted that for a long time." The children are also satisfied with the new marriage. Only the neutral observer has reservations. She feels the following advice is important. "Mrs Reichelt should give herself some time and any decision to get married should be allowed to develop slowly. To forget what is past, she has to forgive, also herself."

Effects

After two months Mrs Reichelt comes in and reports that in past weeks she has not felt so torn inside, even though it "still goes back and forth." She is secure with her second partner and feels closer to him than she did before. In the session that follows, Mrs Reichelt expresses her wish to lay out her sketches again. When she does so she discovers, to her surprise, that her question is no longer which man she belongs with. She experiences a close relationship to the man she lives with and the question of marriage is not important at the moment. What comes out of this for Mrs Reichelt is the realization that each of those involved stand "on their own foundation". As a symbol for this autonomy she adds a sketch of a rectangle. This rectangle turns out to be a dependable resource for her in her ongoing process, a source of strength and energy.

Positive Intentions of Symptoms: Stress as a Helper

Preface

"Re-framing is one of the most important tools of systemic therapy. Literally, the term means giving facts a new framework or putting them in a new context. It leads to a change of perspective, which is the most important requirement for lasting change" (Madelung 1996).

A change of perspective in the next case example is achieved when positive intentions of the symptoms become apparent. "A central premise of systemic procedures is the assumption that a positive intention lies behind every action and behaviour exhibited by a family member, or a part of the personality. This means that every part of a relationship network must be seen as having a right to be there and acknowledged as such" (Madelung 1996). In the next case study, instead of fighting against the primary symptom, an undesirable level of stress, the client works with positive intentions. She recognizes her stress as an aid to keeping herself in balance. This new perspective represents an important step towards a solution to the problem.

What is surely the decisive factor here is that the client develops a new framework out of her own belief system. She finds resolution in connections that appear to her naturally, even when they are not immediately apparent to the therapist.

In this case, a variation of NIG emerges by chance, namely that the client uses abstract symbols (round and rectangular felt pieces) and spatial anchors instead of sketches. Since these felt symbols are usually used for representing a family picture and family constellations, the therapist turns to this element in the following session.

Initial Situation/Problem

Katharina, a sixteen-year-old, finds school easy, with the exception of mathematics, where she has problems. In school she has difficulty paying attention, and studying at home presents concentration problems. When it comes to examinations in this subject, the stress results in a complete mental block and she cannot think clearly.

Issue
Katharina comes for help because she wants to get rid of the stress she experiences with mathematics as she believes that would help her performance in this subject.

Procedure
The therapist asks Katharina to sketch the stress she experiences in connection with maths. She says she would like to colour the entire paper blue. To shorten the process, the therapist offers her a rectangular piece of blue felt, which is normally used for male representatives in a family picture. The client then chooses not to draw any sketches herself, but selects the round, red felt normally used for female representations to stand for her, herself. The therapist asks her to lay the symbols on the floor.

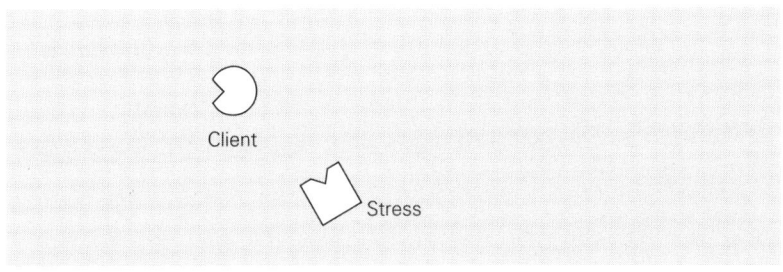

As Katharina stands in her own position, she feels unstable and restless. Her legs move as if she would like to run away. Her left side feels cooler than her right side.

In the position of her stress, on the other hand, she feels fine. The stress, however, is not looking at the client, but past her.

A white piece of felt is added as meta-position, the neutral observer, to look at the relationship of the other two from the outside.

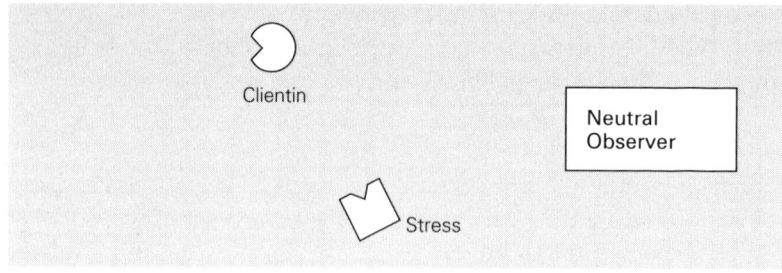

Katharina stands in the position of a neutral observer and determines that the stress wants to be her companion because otherwise she is so alone there. The stress, however, does not feel seen in its place. The therapist asks where the stress is looking. Katharina leaves the meta-position and lays a round, red felt piece in the line of vision of the stress representative. "This is my free time," she explains.

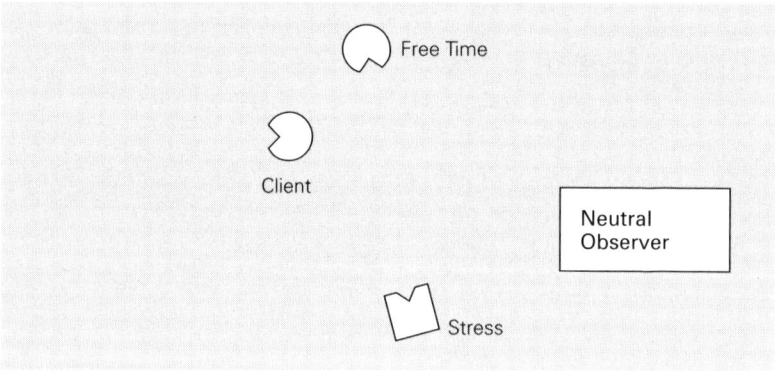

As Katharina stands in the position of the stress, she feels happy that she can see the free time. In her own position, she notices that her left side has become warmer. The question is where she is looking. As an answer, she lays another round, red felt piece on the floor. "This is the free time that I spend with my friends!"

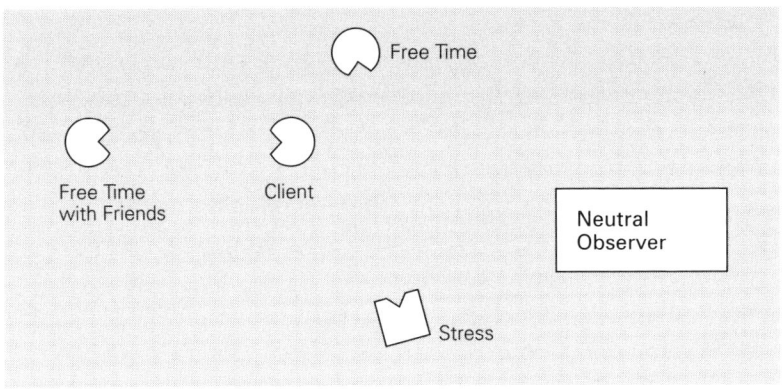

Katharina feels much better in her own position when she can see her free time with her friends. From the position of the neutral observer, she sees that the stress feels even less recognized and also weaker. It sees the situation as "three against one" in relationship to the other positions. The therapist asks the neutral observer for advice so that the stress might feel better. From this position, the neutral observer suggests the following changes:

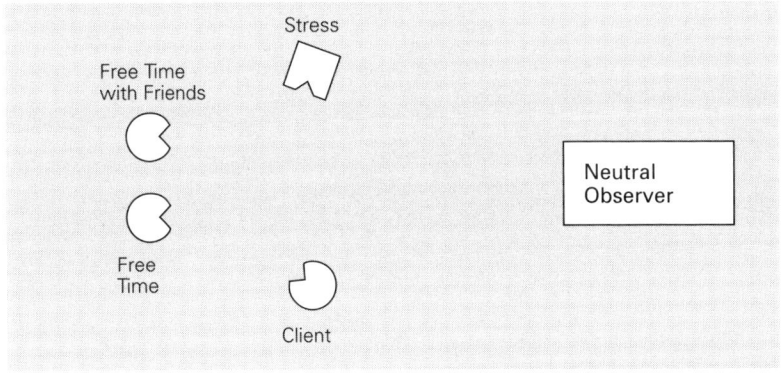

This rearrangement, on the advice of the neutral observer, turns out to be a resolution for all involved. Katharina feels calm and comfortable in her position and sees the stress position as a helper. "My stress takes good care of me. It makes sure that I keep it and my free time in view. Then I'm more balanced." This evaluation is confirmed by the three "helpers". As the client thanks her helpers, she says, "You keep me balanced". The stress in particular feels respected for its efforts and is generally satisfied with the result.

157

Effects

Four weeks later the young client comes back with good news. She did adequately well on her mathematics exam. She used her pre-exam nerves to help her really get into the work of preparation. She admitted that studying even felt like a pleasure, but now she is afraid that she might lose this newly found motivation for maths.

Following Therapy Session

In the first therapy session Katharina chose to use felt pieces usually used to represent people rather than drawing sketches. It occurred to the therapist that the symbols Katharina used corresponded to the number of people in her family and also their gender. Without mentioning the implications from the previous session, the therapist lays the constellation of the resolution out on the floor again. She asks Katharina to try an experiment. "If these pieces of felt were members of your family, who would be standing in which place?" Without hesitation, Katharina assigns the roles.

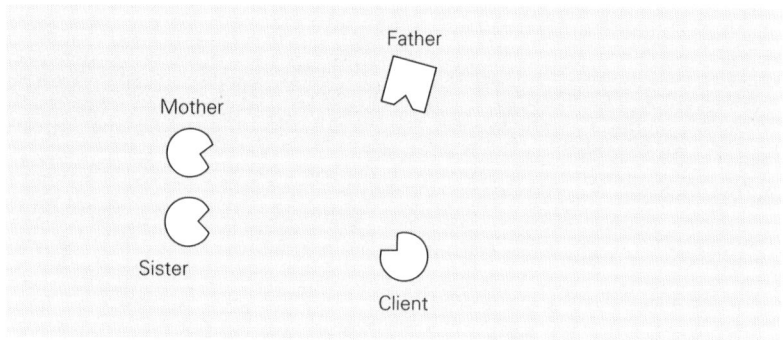

Katharina stands in the position of each family member and discovers that each is looking at a point on the floor that lies between them. In answer to the therapist's questions, the client reports that between her birth and that of her younger sister, her mother had a miscarriage.

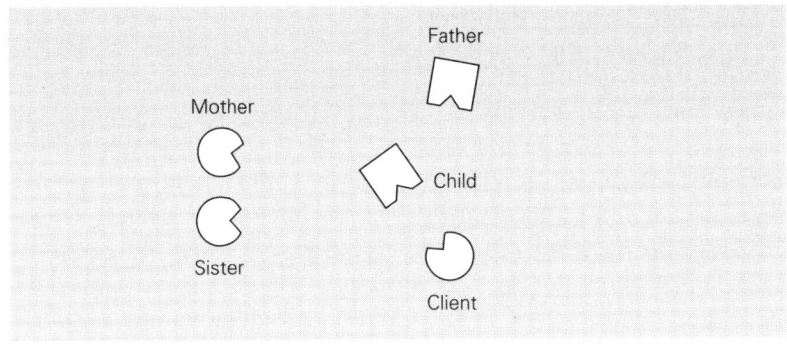

The session continues as the lost child is given a place with its parents, and the two sisters give this child a place in their hearts. The client and all the others represented feel supported and well.

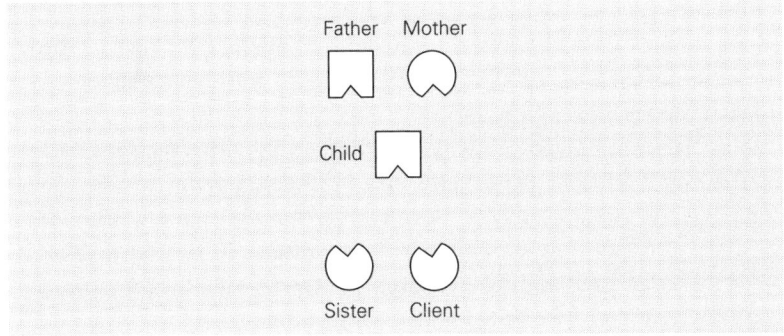

The transformation of the symbols of free time, free time with friends, and stress into family members was not something that had been planned, and was not made a topic of discussion, nor interpreted. It emerged out of the client's fears about losing the positive results of the first therapy session. The fear's corresponding piece was discovered in the lost child, which also provided the resolution. The client did not return to therapy, but her mother reported that her progress in mathematics continued to be satisfactory.

Two Sides: "Solitude and Solidarity", Using Representatives from the Group

Preface

Inner parts of a person are often interwoven with external family members. When we set up our family in a constellation as we see them, we are representing the effects they have on us. That is, when we set up the members of our family, are we not also setting up our inner family, the inner parts of ourselves? Or, vice versa, when we set up parts of ourselves, is this not a mirror image of our relationship to individual family members (cf. p. 30)? Depending on the context and situation, we activate different inner parts of ourselves, and we are "somebody else". For example, in connection with one family member we live out our weak side, or problem side; with another family members, more of our strong or solution- orientated side comes out.

In the next case, the two sides described by the client as her inner divisions are represented by participants in the group. There is a woman representative for solitude, and one for solidarity, or togetherness. They are placed in a constellation along with a representative for the client herself. In the course of the constellation it becomes clear that the client cares for "solitude" like a mother, and even has the feeling of having given birth to this solitude. At the same time, it becomes clear that "solitude" represents the client's mother and the roles are reversed. The daughter is taking care of the mother instead of taking from her (Hellinger 2001). As the work continues, the client is able to leave the solitude, which belongs to her mother, with her mother. She is supported in this by speaking sentences of resolution (Hellinger, Weber a. Beaumont 2001). and by looking at her own son. With the agreement from "solitude", that is, her mother, the client has more chance of seeing "solidarity" as a symbol for her own life and a companion upon her way.

Initial Situation/Problem

Tanja, thirty-three years old, is a participant in a constellation group. She presents her problem as, "I am not myself. I often feel so isolated. Just like my mother. She always complains about her solitary life. But, actually, I have got two sides: The solitary side and the side that likes being together with other people."

Issue

In answer to the question of what a good resolution would be, Tanja says that she would like to know who she is.

Procedure

The therapist asks Tanja to choose three representatives, one for herself, one to represent the solitary side of herself, and one to represent her solidarity with other people.

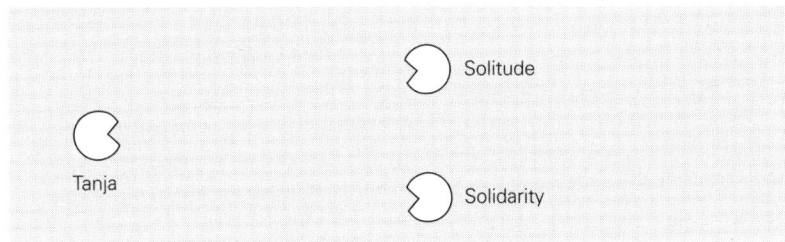

The representatives are asked to feel their way into their roles and then to follow any impulse for movement that they might feel. The following is the result:

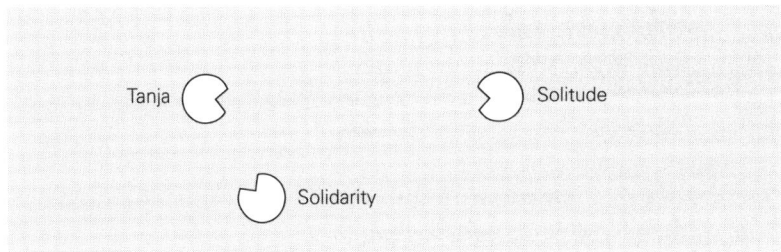

The client's representative has a good feeling about solidarity being there, but also feels drawn towards solitude. Solidarity feels fine. Solitude feels pulled backwards so strongly that it is difficult for her to stand. She kneels down and then sits on the floor. When Tanja's representative sees that, the pull towards solitude increases and she moves to sit behind that representative. The representative of solitude lies down in the client's representative's lap, and feels increasingly sad. Finally she is lying flat on the floor between the legs of Tanja's representative. The therapist asks Tanja to take her own place in the constellation. She immediately has a sense of giving birth to this "solitude".

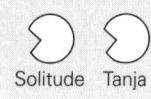

When asked who the solitude might be, Tanja is, at first, very confused. Then, however, she sees that solitude is her mother. The representative of solitude confirms this with a nod.

The therapist asks Tanja to lie down next to her mother on the floor. Tanja weeps and her mother reaches her arms out like a child. The therapist has Tanja say, "Mama, I can't take it away from you." The mother stands up and faces her daughter.

The therapist has Tanja say, "Mama, I am only your child, not your mother. Thank you for giving birth to me and for being as you are. It is difficult for me, but I leave it with you. Now, I am going my own way in my own life." Tanja feels relieved having said this and the therapist moves her to stand next to the representative of solidarity.

In this position, however, Tanja feels unhappy and begins to cry. The therapist has Tanja return to the position facing her mother and say, "Mama, please let me go!" Her mother agrees, but Tanja does not feel convinced. The therapist asks circular questions: "Do you think your mother is happy for you to go your own way?" Since Tanja hesitates, the therapist continues, "Do you think your mother is happy that you have a son and she has a grandson?" Tanja can answer yes to this question wholeheartedly. A representative for her son is added and placed next to her.

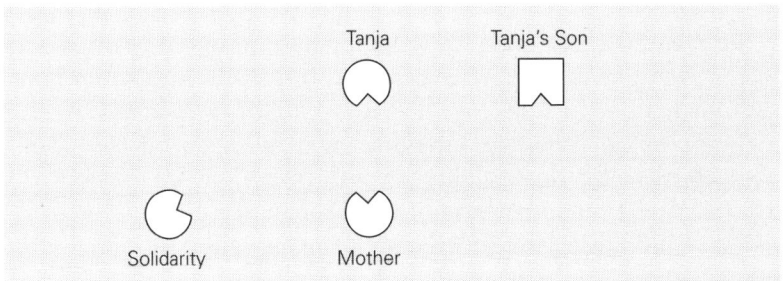

Tanja beams at her mother and says, "Look, Mama, life has continued on. This is your grandson!" All the representatives exhale in relief and the therapist closes the constellation with the words, "And the part with your own life will just take some time."

LINE OF RESOLUTIONS: EVERYONE BELONGS

Preface

This case is an example of how creative and unexpected the course of a therapy session with Neuro-Imaginative Gestalting can be. The therapist first intended to use the basic model of the life path, that is, to move from a sketch of the present problem situation towards an image of the goal with the help of resources. In talking, however, the young client was full of ideas about how to improve his situation, and from the first problem sketch, he developed a continuing row of solution sketches. These sketches build on one another and result in a path to resolution, the last drawing, where the client feels in complete agreement. In the following discussion this solution is also applied to other areas of the client's life.

Initial Situation/Problem

Twelve-year-old Fabian is in the seventh grade. He likes school and was also happy with his own performance up until the end of the sixth grade. Now, three months into the seventh year, he comes for help because he is failing, or almost failing, in every subject, despite great efforts on his part.

Issue

Fabian would like to improve his academic performance.

Procedure

In the therapeutic interview, the following information comes out: Fabian is not aware of any changes or difficulties in his family or with his teachers. In his class, however, a lot has changed. At the beginning of the school year the classes were re-organized. Now there are six boys in his class who are "cool". Although two of them are constantly in trouble because of their behaviour in the classroom, and have been threatened with temporary expulsion from the class, Fabian thinks they are actually quite nice. There are also six other boys in his class who are not so "cool", that he knows and likes from his old class.

The therapist asks Fabian to draw one sketch including the "cool" group, the "not so cool" group, and himself.

Problem in the Present

As Fabian looks at his sketch, he sighs, "Both of them want to go somewhere else. They don't like each other. Holding them together is really hard work!" The impression of strenuous effort is confirmed when Fabian lays the sketch on the floor and stands on it. His arms feel very heavy and he feels torn apart. He doesn't know where he belongs.

The therapist suggests that he draw a picture in which things are less taxing for him.

Solution 1

"Here I'm always running back and forth between the two", comments Fabian, as he looks at this picture. He lays the sketch on the floor above the sketch of the problem in the present and stands on the new sketch. "No, that's not any easier. I'm tired from all the running back and forth." The therapist asks him if he has any other ideas about what would make it easier for him.

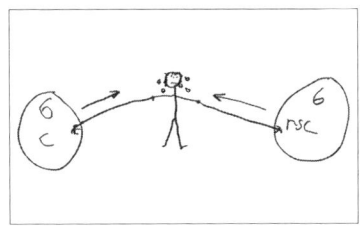

Solution 2

"Now I'm just taking my lasso and pulling them in towards me. I want them to be together!" This picture is laid on the floor above the first solution, continuing the line. When Fabian stands on this sketch, he notices how tiring this solution also is. He stands, with his shoulders and body drooping, devoid of energy. When asked what would happen if he didn't hold these two groups together any more, Fabian sits down and draws his answer on the next paper.

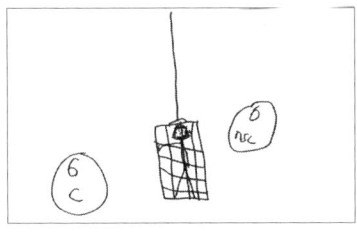

Solution 3

"If I don't hold them together, they are very far apart and I am locked in", he remarks as he looks at this picture. When he lays this paper on the floor and stands in this position, he is aware of how sad this situation makes him feel. He returns to the drawing surface, murmuring, "No, that's too sad. I'll draw something else."

Solution 4

Fabian explains his drawing. "Here are some brake chocks that keep the cool ones and the not so cool ones in their places. Now I'm fine!" He lays this sketch in the row of pictures. When he stands on this drawing, he feels lighter and stronger than in the other positions. However, doubts begin to creep into his chest area and he asks, a bit discouraged, "What happens if they just take away the chocks?"

When he returns to the drawing table, the therapist sits down with him and they consider, together, if there isn't something besides wheel chocks that could hold his old friends and new friends together. They discuss the fact that there are also twelve girls in the class and that the class was given a new name at the beginning of the year, namely 7B. When asked to draw the class and its new name, Fabian suddenly comes to life. With fluid strokes he draws an oval, hangs a 7B sign on it and with no hesitation he gives everybody a place in the class: Himself, the girls (M = Mädchen), the "cool" group, and the "not so cool" group.

Visibly relieved, Fabian looks at the various groups that are clearly separate from one another, but also connected to each other. Rather abruptly he says, "Now I'll get my lasso out again." As the therapist looks at him, puzzled, since the lasso hadn't proven very effective at holding the groups together in the previous sketch, Fabian smiles mischievously. "So I can rope myself some good marks (Gute Noten)!" As he lays this drawing at the end of the row of sketches and stands on it, it is clear that he is in agreement with this solution. He stands up straight and relaxed and says, "Yeah, it's fine like that!"

166

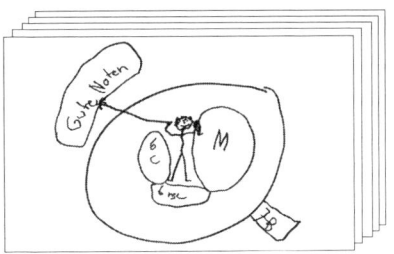

Good Solution

The therapist asks Fabian to go back to the beginning of the row of solution pictures and collect each picture. He makes a stack of the sketches with the good solution on top and stands on the whole packet. "Now I'm strong," he comments, and looks around the room eagerly.

Finally, the therapist asks Fabian about what other groups he knows of where everyone has a place whether they like each other or not. He mentions the judo team, the football team, the whole school, and his father in his office. The therapist mentions that in families it is also true that even if everyone doesn't always get on with everyone else, they still all belong to the family.

Effects

In the following session, the therapist works with Fabian using some kinesiology exercises for the integration of the right and left sides of the brain. This anchors the process at the neurological level (cf. p. 130). At half term, his mother reports that although Fabian has not quite reached his prior performance level, he is on his way. He has energy and motivation for his studies and has been elected class representative.

CASE EXAMPLE: EVA MADELUNG: LINE OF RESOLUTIONS

The following case study consists of a client's report of her experience and the therapist's record of the work with Doris. Since the two reports supplement one another, sections of each are numbered correspondingly.

The Client's Report

1) In March, for the first time, I was finally going to be able to accompany my husband on a business trip and we were going to Paris. My mother had come to take care of the three children and we had made it through the last work day. My mother asked me to phone my niece to make arrangements with her for the upcoming family Easter holiday at my father's house.

For a long time I got only a busy signal, and when I finally reached her, her voice sounded very thin. She said she had some bad news for me. Her father (my brother) had committed suicide by hanging himself. My niece's fiancé had found my brother in his house after they hadn't been able to reach him for two days.

"To feel the stillness of death." For days I was withdrawn into my own centre as never before. I was shocked at myself at how little I cried, and how factually I told others about it.

During the Whitsun holidays, I bought some books about suicide and while reading them I finally started to cry. I had a lot of free time since my husband was taking care of our children.

For at least half a year I had difficulty sleeping, and I had very intense dreams involving my brother. These dreams stayed with me long into the following day. I kept thinking about things like: How far under must he be? How dark and hopeless does the situation have to get to enable you, or force you to take such an enormous step? What did our parents do wrong that they didn't give us any structure for managing crises? Was I making the same mistake with my own children? Did I have enough to be able to give them something? Would they even come to me? What did I do in crisis situations?

The answers to my questions were devastating. I became very forgetful and I was only able to manage the bare essentials around the house before running out of energy. Suddenly I started to wonder why my husband would want to stay with a loser like me. One afternoon, when I had just had a row with my youngest daughter in which I once again came out on the losing end, I felt a compulsion to hurt myself. I wanted to either cut my arm with a knife or beat my head against the wall until it bled. I wanted to give my inner pain an outer expression. The extent of the danger was not really clear to me, as I was hardly aware of myself. Our middle daughter stood next to me and worriedly stroked my back.

Our youngest daughter (M) suffered the most, but still fought against any demands from me. She developed homesickness, which she had never had before. First she had to be picked up from a farm where she was on holiday with friends. Later, she couldn't stay overnight with friends, and then even a few hours in the afternoon was too much. Finally I got a call at work one morning at 8:30 that I had to pick M up from school. She was crying and couldn't be comforted. She wanted her mama. It was then really clear that something had to be done. M, at age nine, was already in play therapy and the psychologist told me that M was worried about me. She couldn't let me out of her sight for fear I would simply disappear.

I had to do something about myself! But where should I turn?

I knew E. M. from a brief therapy years ago, and knew I wouldn't have to start telling my story from the very beginning with her. I also knew I could expect help from her quickly.

First Session

2) I sat in a large wingback armchair and rested my head on the back. I was feeling so exhausted. After I had told her about the current situation, E asked me to draw a picture of my problem with my left, non-dominant hand.

Picture 1

I explained the picture to E: "I am standing in the middle covered by a black bell jar. My family have to support me. My youngest daughter (small figure to the right) is pulling at me. I feel an additional duty to my family of origin (because of my brother's death) and for my sister-in-law, who is facing complete ruin after a year and a half of marriage to my brother (grave with cross and figure). Is death a temptation for me? (Grave with coloured flowers). On top of that come some heavy thoughts about my work, which also has to do with people (figures on the right at the top) who need my help."

E: "How does your husband see your situation? How is it at work? It's clearly better for you there. It's easy to see that you sit up straight and your face relaxes when you talk about that."

3) We talk about the systemic connections that might have something to do with my brother's suicide: Connections with the Nazi time, possibly guilt that he took on from the system. A family constellation might give a clearer impression. Even though there might not be a clear indication of the reason for his suicide, I could still get a broader view of the whole thing in a larger context, which might give me some relief.

Before the next session I am to gather information about my grandfather's involvement and/or possible guilt.

E: "Draw a picture of a state in the future in which this current problem has been resolved, or you have learned to deal with it."

So, what do I want, actually? I haven't thought about that for a long time. I have been caught up in how terrible everything is.

It should stop hurting so much when I think about my brother. How do you draw that? What colour should I choose? I had better not think about it so much, just choose a colour spontaneously. Don't put myself under any pressure. The picture is only for me anyway. I can take my time, all the time in the world, all the time I need.

What do I want for myself? I want to be able to stand on my own again without my family's help. They shouldn't have to worry about me. But I want to be in contact with them and I want to be able to talk openly with the children about their uncle's death. I don't want to forget him, but he should be more in the background and not always interfering in my everyday life. My concern for my relatives should also fade into the background.

Picture 2

When she asks, I tell Eva my thoughts about this picture.

E: "What would help you to get to this goal? Draw a picture."

What do I need? If I knew what I needed I wouldn't need help! In these diffuse images and thoughts I have to force myself to focus and stay concrete. What has helped me up until now? I am familiar with this way of thinking from my first encounter with this method: Building on what has already been mastered. I had forgotten about it, though, and now in this situation, looking at my blank paper, I remember it again.

4) It has always been easiest for me when I have a clear goal to aim towards. Exactly! A smile comes to my face, the first in how long? I need a clear goal again!

Ziel = Goal

Picture 3

I have a feeling of relief. Strange, I know this procedure, but alone, it was impossible for me to ask myself these simple questions. Simple questions but it's already brought something positive. I have hope again. From now on, the way is up!

Second Session

5) I talk about what I have been able to find out about my ancestors and about a particularly powerful dream:

6) I saw Fritz coming towards me in the marketplace and thought, "Now I'm having hallucinations, too!" He offered to buy me a cake and go somewhere for coffee. I said, "We can't do that, you're dead." He answered, "I just wanted to be alone for a while. Now I'm here again. Let's go!" I said, "Nobody wants to have coffee with you. That doesn't work. You can't just pretend that nothing has happened. None of us can live like we used to." At that, he looked very touched. "I'm sorry about that. I just wanted to be alone." Orange blood ran out of his heart onto his white t-shirt.

Third Session

7) After an initial talk, E asked: "What has helped you to reach your goals in the past?"

From a jumble of feelings and thoughts the first step becomes discernible. What do I need now to get back on my feet? What would be good for me? Do I need some time out? Support? If yes, then from who?

And also: What is going well for us? What have we already achieved? What am I grateful for? Then I have strength again. The thing I feel most grateful for is the love I get from my husband. After so many years of marriage, I finally have the feeling that I have enough love, I'm even satiated sometimes, and not always so needy.

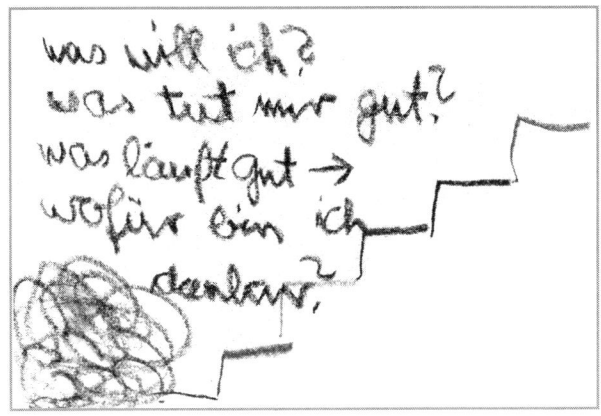

was will ich? = What do I want?
was tut mir gut? = What is doing me good?
was läuft gut = What is going well?
wofür bin ich dankbar? = What am I grateful for?

Picture 4

E: "How do you know that you have got enough now? Draw a picture."

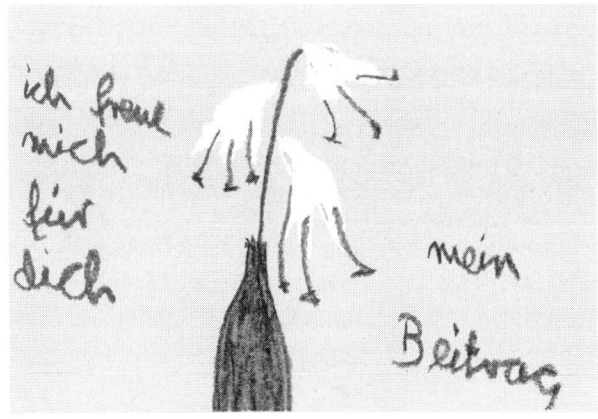

ich freue mich für dich = I am happy for you
mein Beitrag = My contribution

Picture 5: Able to give

There was a very concrete situation in which I can see it. My husband got promoted to head of his department. When he told me about it, my first reaction was annoyance. I was annoyed that he was making a career "at my cost". At my cost meant to me that he would work more overtime, he would have more obligations, and therefore, would be less support at home, so I would come out on the short end (as usual).

At first I hardly reacted to him at all. I didn't say anything about my negative reaction. I brooded about it for a few days and then I asked myself: "If I were promoted, how would I like my husband to react?" I would want joy and rejoicing, at least a bottle of champagne! In any event, certainly not blame! As of that moment, I began to change my attitude. My husband deserves to have me feel happy for him and with him, and to value his professional achievements. As a result, I bought a lily and set it on his bed table with a short letter. Since then, there has been more love flowing in me and I have become aware that I have something to give and don't always have to be in the "victim" role.

E: "That's a part of growing up. You've changed since the last time we met."

Yes, that's true. I'm not nearly as uncertain and anxious as when E. first got to know me. I know what I want and now I can usually take good care of myself.

I had a homework assignment to continue to look for additional sources of strength and sketch them. I brought them to the session.

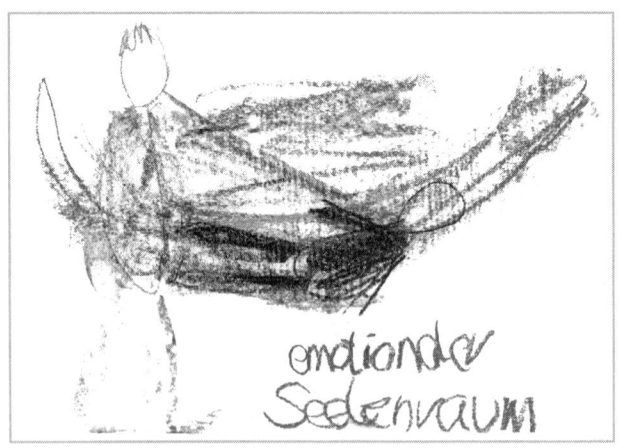

emotionaler Seelenraum = emotional 'soul-space'

Picture 6: A skill: Educational work with children

174

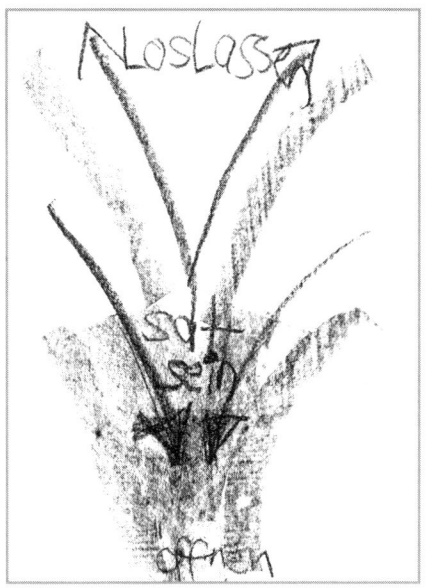

loslassen = setting free
satt sein = replete/full
öffnen = opening

Picture 7: Secure in my relationship with my husband and children

Vision = Vision
Beruf = Profession
Arbeitsstelle = Job

Finanzen = Finances
Haus = House
Partner = Partner

Picture 8: Family and professional goals

Gottvertrauen = Trust in God

Picture 9: Trust in God

8) I had a wonderful experience doing my homework. As I was getting out my drawing supplies, M was very curious and asked what I was going to do. I told her about my homework assignment. She sat down with me and said she wanted to do that kind of homework, too. She drew enthusiastically and when we were finished, we told each other something about our pictures. It gave her a bit of strength and it brought the two of us closer together.

9) E: "Where are you now? Do you have any sense of having come closer to your goal, or has your goal changed in the meantime? Draw a picture."

Picture 10

This picture means that my family do not have to support me anymore, but we are still holding hands. I still need close contact. I have a second shell around me that expresses my feeling of vulnerability. My husband is standing between me and M., so she won't keep clinging on to me. He is trying to pay more attention to her because he is more stable at the moment and he wants to give me some relief. My family of origin is not a burden to me at the moment. I have the feeling that they can also stand alone again.

The grave is still there, but it isn't so tempting and full of flowers.

E: "Lay out the pictures and see how it looks now."

(She lays out the papers and stands in the position of the present.)

10) "In general, I feel fine. I am very close to reaching my goal. I don't feel burdened anymore, I can stand, I feel my strength again and I'm full of self-confidence."

E: "Do you want another appointment or do you think this is sufficient for the moment and that you can deal with things yourself?"

After a slight hesitation and checking out my inner state, I answer: "No, I would like another appointment because my current feelings seem so fragile. I'm worried that I am not strong enough yet."

My homework assignment is to remember meaningful experiences in which I had a feeling of being in the right place in the world and to draw them.

Fourth Session

Picture 11: Power of the Sea

177

11) I explain that the picture shows the power of the sea, something I experienced during my last holiday. The waves crash tirelessly against the rocks with full force. I want to have a tiny bit of this power.

E: "Have you got other memories like this?"

I had a similar experience going for a walk when there were storm warnings up. The force of the wind awakened a desire for power in me, and a life full of energy and vitality.

Picture 12: Walk in a storm

Finally, E asked me to sketch the current situation.

Picture 13: Looser than before; family as a circle

I laid all the pictures I had drawn so far in a kind of life path, enriched by resources along the side. I walked slowly along this path and felt once again each phase I had been through. I could feel what it means to have my resources clearly in front of me where I can see them and feel them. I felt strong enough to take over my everyday life again.

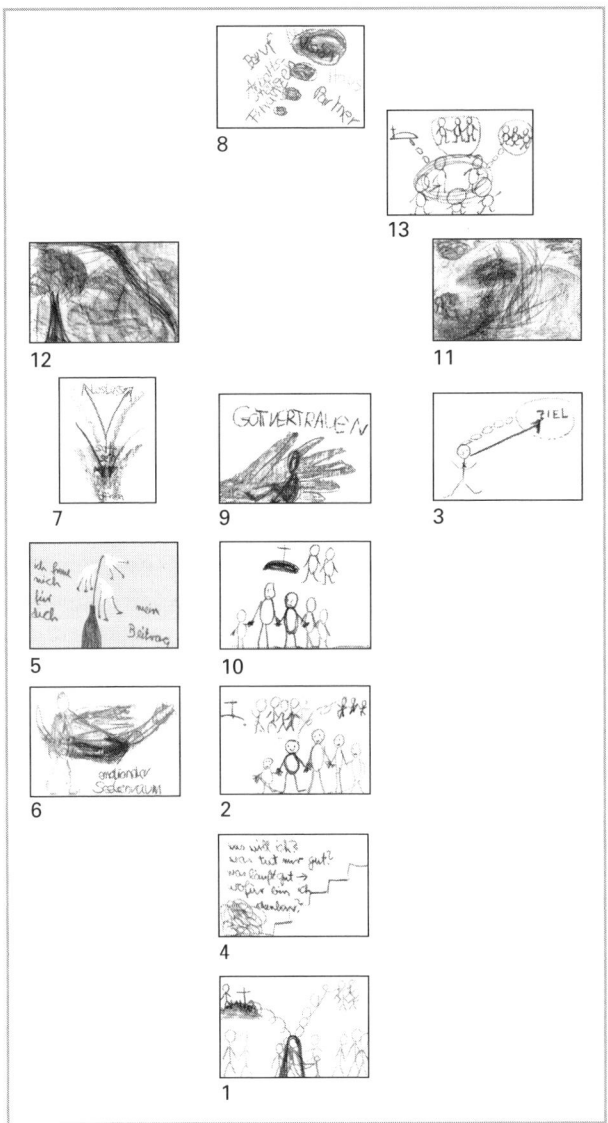

Picture 14: End Configuration

At my last appointment we didn't continue the whole session because my goal of being able to act had been reached. Beyond the goal I had set, I had also found joy and delight in life.

The Therapist's Report

First Session

1) Doris was in therapy some years ago, and has now returned. In the intervening time she has had three daughters, and has returned to work again. She is happy in her marriage. Her brother committed suicide six months ago, and this event precipitated a deep depression, much worse than anything Doris has ever experienced before. She is exhausted and cannot manage her family duties. At the moment she feels unable to work and has taken a leave of absence.

2) In the initial interview she reports that she had been at her lowest point two weeks earlier when she phoned for a therapy appointment (picture 1). Since then she has improved somewhat. The therapist asks her what she thinks has contributed to this improvement.

Doris: First of all, my husband helped a lot. Secondly, I went to a homeopath who prescribed something to resolve the shock condition. Thirdly, I tried to get in touch with what was happening to everybody else. I can function again now. Besides that, I can really feel my husband's love and I have had some good talks with my eldest daughter (who had been very problematic some years ago). I can feel the love in my surroundings again.

3) Her mother and father have been separated for twenty years. Her mother lost her own father when she was twelve. Doris' father lost two of his brothers in the war. "It had to be me, the good-for-nothing, who survived," he sometimes said. She has three siblings. Her brother was married twice and drank a lot. Two weeks before his suicide, he fell out of a window, but had only minor injuries, and it was described as an accident. When asked about her concept of a resolution in the future, she drew picture 2.

4) The therapist suggests the exercise of looking for resources along a life path for the next session. Doris is familiar with this exercise from her own training. She agrees and, in closing, makes a sketch of her present situation, picture 3.

As she is leaving, she comments with a smile, "I know this work, but in a situation like this you just can't do it alone."

Second Session

The situation has improved. Additional facts from her family of origin have emerged. Her father's father was an "idealistic" Nazi party member. Following some disagreement concerning the company IG-Farben, he was sent to Auschwitz. She doesn't know anything more about that event.

5) She describes a powerful dream about her brother. The therapists emphasizes how important it is for her to confront him, and thereby also   herself, with the reality of his death. She mentions that many in the family have dreamt about her brother. She also says that her youngest daughter was present when she got the news on the telephone about her brother's death. This daughter is exhibiting signs of anxiety at the moment and is very defiant. Doris is given the homework assignment of looking for resources.

Third Session

Doris brings in pictures 6, 7, 8, and 9. She says that she didn't find the time to work on the resources until the evening before this session. Her youngest daughter was present and asked her what she was doing. She explained that she was doing her homework, and told her daughter what the task was. Her daughter decided she wanted to do it, too. They worked together for a long time and her daughter drew pictures of situations in which she is competent.

6) The therapist has Doris sketch an image of the present. Doris notices that her current situation has changed since the last time in the direction of her concept of the goal (picture 10).

7) The homework assignment is to continue to draw additional pictures of resources together with her daughter, and to talk with her daughter about how she imagines it is now for her uncle.

Fourth Session

8) She is doing well and the pressure has let up. She did not draw with her daughter but she did talk with her about her uncle. "He is sitting in the clouds, and flies around from one person in the family to another."

The therapist suggests that when an opportunity arises, she should mention to her daughter that her uncle is happy when he sees that things are going well for her.

Doris is asked to draw a new sketch of the present situation. She notices that this picture and the picture of the image of the goal are very similar (picture 13). She lays out all the pictures as it now seems right. The resulting configuration is as in picture 14.

She stands on each of the resources again, looks at the whole picture from the outside position, and ends the exercise.

In the accompanying report from Doris about her experiences, she says that working with her daughter on the pictures of life resources had amazing results.

Commentary

The thread that runs through this series of sessions is clear – finding resources from the course of the client's life, as described on p. 77, this therapeutic element is appropriate for crisis situations of a physical or psychological nature. It should be noted that the actual follow-through of collecting the resources and taking them along into the present was superfluous here. In a certain sense, the life path laid out spontaneously at the end also represents the various stages in the course of the therapy.

In the first session, the idea of sketching the situation as an image of the direction towards a goal was probably prompted by the question about what had helped to improve the situation. On the other hand, familiarity with the therapeutic element of the "life path" surely played a role here.

The systemic connections did not need to be represented symbolically, as they were present in reality in the form of her uncle, her daughter, her husband, memories of her father and grandfather, and in her dreams.

The role played by the client's brother for her and for other members of the family reflected a dynamic often seen in family constellations around the influence exerted on the family by someone who has died in unusual circumstances.

Perhaps the goal of being able to function was realized in such a logical and consistent way because it was concretely appropriate and systemically orientated to the client's situation as a wife and mother. Additionally, reaching the goal was made possible by letting go and resisting the dead brother's tendency to hang on. This corresponds to the archaic orders of relationship.

Time span: Seven weeks, approximately 14 day intervals between sessions.

10. The Existential Paradox

Two Kinds of Reality?

We will now turn back from our focus on practice in order to look more deeply into the theoretical background of this work.

The original systemic therapies, such as the family therapy approach developed at the Mental Research Institute (MRI) in Palo Alto, California, by the Gregory Bateson circle; NLP; de Shazer's systemic brief therapy; and the Milan and Heidelberg schools of family therapy; these, are all based upon so-called constructivism. This premise assumes that individuals create their own reality. Anyone with a background in therapy approaches of this kind is familiar with the dictum originally from Corzipsky and often repeated by Bateson, "The map is not the territory". From this perspective, therapy is an attempt to change the client's viewpoint in order to adjust the inner "map" (imaginary world) to correspond to current circumstances. In Germany it has become customary to group the above named therapy approaches under the term "systemic-constructivist".

At the beginning of the nineties, demand rose for Bert Hellinger's family constellation work. In this approach, the focus is on reality as it is manifested to us, that is, the unchangeable givens in our lives. For example, our parents are and will always remain our parents, and life is passed on to us through them. Leaning in the direction of the philosophical concept of phenomenology, Bert Hellinger called his approach "systemic-phenomenological".

The first publication on this method, *Zweierlei Glück – die systemische Psychotherapie Bert Hellingers*, edited by Gunthard Weber, (Weber 1993) became a bestseller. This book has been re-worked for the English edition *"Love's Hidden Symmetry"* by Hunter Beaumont in co-operation with Bert Hellinger (2001). At the same time, controversy developed in professional circles as to whether a therapy that replaces the constructivist viewpoint with a phenomenological one could even be called systemic. Those interested in the potential for psychological help offered by this method remained unaffected by the discussion and their numbers continued to increase.

Since that time, both viewpoints have been represented in the systemic therapy scene. If we look carefully at Bateson's map metaphor, it is clear that besides the map we create on our own, there is also a territory according to which the map is drawn. Does this mean that this early thinker of systemic constructivist methods secretly, or actually rather openly, was also looking at a manifested reality that has an interactive effect with the created reality? That this is so becomes clear primarily in his last, posthumously published book, *"Angels Fear. Towards an Epistemology of the Sacred"* (Bateson a. Bateson 1987).

Variable and Immutable: Two Sides of One Coin

The two viewpoints represented in systemic therapy are increasingly no longer mutually exclusive but rather complementary, which corresponds to the nature of the polarities of our own psychological make up. One could say, using the computer metaphor, that the phenomenological approach is "hardware" focussed, and the constructivist approach is concerned with improving the "software". One looks at the immutable facts of life and the other tends to the variables.

These two ways of seeing things could be called Siamese twins, or two sides of the same coin. Herein lies an old and still unanswered question that has occupied philosophers, certainly since Kant, but probably since the Scholastics, or even the Pre-Socratics, with no consensus or agreement yet about how real reality is or what is real. It is, therefore, most valuable to have both modes of thought represented in systemic therapy.

Belonging and Autonomy

Another Siamese twin pair is the polarity of belonging and autonomy. Clearly there is a close relationship between these two pairs. Belonging is related to the "manifested" reality and autonomy to the "created" reality. This means that a person for whom belonging is more in the foreground experiences himself as a part of something larger, a part of a "given" reality. Another, for whom striving towards autonomy has priority, feels drawn to the metaphors of "shaping" one's life, or constructed reality. These two attitudes may change in the course of a lifetime though they can be life-long determinants.

During childhood, belonging is naturally the foreground issue. Depending on whether the experiences are more positive or negative, the phase of separation is made easier or more difficult. Those who have experienced belonging in a good way usually have an easier time separating at an appropriate age and forming new relationships than do those who had to rely on themselves as children and have not had the experience of belonging to a stable parental relationship. Sometimes, however, they are precisely the people capable of a special kind of creativity in their lives. Here, too, we can see the paradoxical interplay of the polarities (cf. Bischof 200).

THE ASPECTS OF BELONGING AND AUTONOMY IN THERAPEUTIC APPROACHES

Family constellations, as developed by Bert Hellinger, focus primarily on the aspect of belonging. Experience has shown that a person who acknowledges the archaic orders of relationships manifested in a constellation becomes more able to find a position of separateness that is good for everyone. In hypnotherapy, on the other hand, a pioneer of systemic therapy, Milton H. Erickson, focuses on the urge towards separation or striving for autonomy. Just as primary love in a relationship network can produce entanglements with destructive effects, so, too, a defiant, "desperate attempt to define oneself" can lead to self-destruction (Erickson 1980).

MANIFEST REALITY AND CREATED REALITY IN EVERYDAY EXPERIENCES

Looking at reality as it is manifested or as it is created are two therapeutic orientations, but our concrete everyday experience includes both at the same time.

At some point in our lives, who amongst us hasn't felt the need to take things in hand and move in our own direction, act independently, or just do something different from our parents? We sometimes have an experience of finally reaching a much desired goal that means we have been able to shape our lives appropriately. At other times, however, what is most apparent is a sense of our interconnectedness with a larger network, whether it is expressed as a feeling of security and support, or as a sense of helpless despair. We may feel cared for and supported or helpless and at the mercy of others.

Taking responsibility for ourselves and being integrated in a network are clearly two basic feeling states, or ways of looking at life. Our life swings back and forth between the two, and we sometimes experience both at once. For example, when we feel proud of ourselves for having finally reached a desired goal after much effort, but at the same time we are aware of how many other people and external circumstances have contributed to our success.

In addition, it would seem that, as a basic determinant in their lives, some people tend to look in one direction, others in the other direction. There are "doers", who in their robust self-confidence tend to forget that they have had help along the way from others. On the other hand, there are "losers" who don't believe themselves capable of any achievement or who always blame others for their woes. There are also those who live life with a kind of artistry, combining both aspects in a flexible way, and transforming unfavourable circumstances into positives, sometimes to their own amazement. And then there are those who, in piety, surrender to a greater power, who take things as they find them and either draw strength from what comes their way or who avoid facing up to the challenge. There are, of course, countless ways of combining these two approaches to life.

EXISTENTIAL PARADOX AND THE PARADOXICAL STRUCTURE OF THE SOUL

When we think back on difficult situations in our lives that were dealt with well, it is usually clear that both approaches were present, the feeling of being connected to the whole *and* the independent will to act; the feeling of helplessness *and* the drive to succeed; the yielding to others *and* taking responsibility for ourselves.

Reality manifested and reality created, "the two sides of the coin" are apparently inseparable in an existential paradox that corresponds to the paradoxical structure of the soul.

This paradoxical structure points to a view of people in which the development of the ego function, so important to the western way of thinking, is also connected to an awareness that we are part of a greater whole.

Bert Hellinger formulated it as follow:

"Some think they are searching for the truth of their own soul. But, in reality, the greater soul thinks and searches through us."

11. The Limited Value of Theoretical Considerations

"Phenomenology means sacrificing our desire for understanding in favour of recognizing reality." This is Bert Hellinger's formulation of his viewpoint that awareness takes priority over ideas.

Actually, every understanding is a construct, insofar as it is the product of our capacity to know, which is dependent upon certain conditions and is, therefore, limited. There are not only intellectual pre-conditions, which occupy a central place in Kant's thinking, but also pre-conditions of a psychological nature, which would include, for example, Jung's archetypes. More recently, the philosopher Karl-Otto Apel has spoken of "Leibapriori der Erkenntnis", the a priori physical nature of cognition (Apel 1986). He means that everything in our awareness and the way we process it, is determined by our nervous system and brain function. Following this through to the end, we come to the conclusion that both human realities, what is created as well as what is manifested, must conform to the "human", to the "brain". This puts limitations on both the constructivist and phenomenological approaches, as long as they are contained within the human body. The one may see itself as the discoverer of a "virtual" world subject to change according to wish and technical ability, and the other may see itself as capable of directly "seeing" reality or even truth, but the dependence upon our apparatus of knowing – our brain and nervous system – cannot be denied. Both have to acknowledge that their capabilities are limited by physiological, psychological, and intellectual givens.

Scientific research in cognition has shown that the brain is forced to choose from an unlimited supply of available information in order to put together a reality that is reasonably manageable. This means that our own awareness conforms to human constraints, since we cannot be aware of anything that isn't available to us through our senses. In addition, we only recognize those things we can imagine, even if it is only a very rudimentary idea. An example from everyday life is what happens when you have been searching high and low for something but can't find it. Finally, when you have given up hope, it appears, and indeed in one of the places you have already looked. It is clear that you overlooked the exact thing you were looking for because you had an incorrect image in mind. The interplay between images and awareness becomes clear (cf. p. 21).

Further, an interest in the scientific study of cognition cannot ignore how little we actually know about the functioning of this wonderful organ, the brain, and how far we still are from being able to intervene creatively to alter its functions (despite banner headlines repeatedly heralding progress in this direction).

The Brain: "Just" for Survival?

Bert Hellinger's statement, quoted at the beginning of this chapter, alerts us to a danger. Striving for theoretical understanding may impair our capacity for awareness. Too much clarity disrupts our awareness and reality eludes an overly firm grasp of understanding. Hellinger once commented, "We reach for the shining truth and hardly notice that it limits, blinds, and encloses us. The dark truth, dim around the edges is more exact. It makes us alert so that we open up all our senses, just as we do when moving in the dark."

On the other hand, our desire for understanding has been scientifically documented (Spitzer 2003). Our endocrine system releases endorphins, "feel-good" hormones, when we have understood something or believe we have understood something. We certainly would not wish to lose this by shutting down our desire for understanding – which would be difficult to do in any case. Knowing this, however, warns us against taking our understanding of something for the truth of the matter. Our brain is probably an instrument designed more for survival than for understanding. What does this mean in terms of Bert Hellinger's "orders of love" (Hellinger, Weber a. Beaumont 2001)? Can they be basically valid and have effects on us, regardless of whether or not we know about and acknowledge them? Or, are they Hellinger's constructs, as many believe? The followers of the Heidelberg School would maintain, that families have specific standards of relationship, that are renegotiable at certain times.

As far as I know, Hellinger has never said that the orders of love represent objective truths. He is speaking more of innate orders of relationship that drive us to ensure survival. They grew out of a time when people lived together in hordes and the brain proved its value as an instrument of survival. An act against the order and exclusion from the community could mean death. The archaic orders of love have to do with a reality formed within human conditions, namely that of our family relationships. Within this reality, the orders have validity.

Nonetheless, particularly within a phenomenological approach, we should remain open to awareness of something new and different, "sacrificing our desire for understanding in favour of recognizing reality".

UNDERSTANDING?

De Shazer has also expressed deep scepticism regarding our capacity for understanding. "There is no understanding. There are only more or less useful misunderstandings" (spoken comment).

Viewed precisely, this statement is not as brusque as it might appear at first glance. He is not saying that there is no communication between people. He is only warning us against any illusion that "understanding" someone means understanding another person in detail. A word to the wise for all those who believe in their capacity for empathy as a reliable instrument for discovering the truth, and those who think they can understand another person better than that person understands himself.

We can regard this, admittedly somewhat curt, dismissal as an indication of the endless variety in human realities, which we participate in but can never fully comprehend.

UNDERLYING METAPHORS AS THEORY FOR FAMILY CONSTELLATIONS

In accordance with the above statements, Bert Hellinger has largely avoided forming any theory about the methods he has developed. I say "largely" because theoretical leanings are visible in his repeated use of terms from the philosopher Martin Heidegger, or parallels in the poems of Rainer Maria Rilke. Even though these indications appear only in periodic quotes, they point to a grounding of his own awareness through the similar or parallel views and experiences of well-known poets and thinkers such as Rilke and Heidegger.

We can see these indicators as underlying metaphors that serve as a basis for practice that focuses directly on awareness. In this way, metaphors such as "orders of love" or the "greater soul" encompass observations of repeated phenomena in vivid descriptive terms that guide awareness in a certain direction and support practice. In using descriptions that are not as sharply delineated, awareness is less constricted than is the case when using a logical, precisely defined term.

We can conclude these considerations, which warn of too much consideration, with a view from another continent. Malidoma Somé explains a Dagara expression in his book *Of Water and the Spirit* (1994). "*Yielbogura* is the thing that cannot be eaten by knowledge … The word says that the very life and power of some things come from their resistance to the categorizing that is commonly applied to everything these days".

NLP's Grounding in Cognitive Science

It has been said repeatedly that NLP is based on a reality that is created, whereas family constellation work is based on a reality that is manifested. It has also been detailed in this book how these two ways of seeing the world complement one another. The differences, however, are such that, at first glance, a complementary application of both methods would seem to be impossible.

A glance at the NLP literature reveals the differences immediately. Scientific terms of behaviour and models such as the TOTE (Test-Operate-Test-Exit) model (see Dilts, Bandler and Grinder 1985) are used as a basis for practice. There are polished, step-by-step therapeutic strategies, and the feeling is one of being in an engineering office of psychological construction. At the same time, the extent to which the unconscious goes along with it is astounding. Surprisingly, this is often the case.

This emphasis on a clear theoretical foundation corresponds to the hierarchy of ideas in the therapeutic process of NLP. Even though the awareness of minimal physiological reactions of the client plays a great role, the primary concern is adjusting the mental images formed earlier, in other circumstances, to match the current reality and to direct them in a positive vein. You could look at NLP as advanced training in the skills of dealing with images and concepts in shaping and creating one's life. The results can be valuable in everyday life.

This concept does not include the possibility that a deceased family member whom the client did not even know could play any significant role, since it is concerned with influences from the biographical level (cf. Stresius, Castella, and Grochowiak 2002).

Such experiences are relegated to a realm in which only *Acknowledging What Is* (Hellinger and ten Hövel 1999) is of help, an area where the very foundation of concepts such as "gestalting" life or "human engineering" are called into question. Once again we see a glimmer of the existential paradox taking shape.

PRACTICAL VALUE OF THEORY

In spite of all these considerations, we consider a certain basis of theoretical knowledge to be important. The understanding that arises from practice and serves practice can support therapeutic independence and serve creativity. In this sense, what has been said in the theoretical chapters should provide a framework for therapeutic practice, but, should also be informed and enriched by experiences from practice. We believe that an independent and creative use of any method requires a thorough theoretical understanding *and* practical experience.

12. Closing Discourse

BARBARA INNECKEN: THE TWO TREES

At the beginning of this book I described how I got acquainted with Neuro-Imaginative Gestalting during a summer holiday in southern Italy, and how I came to learn the method through my own experiences and through supervision. To round things off, I'd like to tell you about my first session with Eva Madelung.

In the meantime it had turned to winter and the Christmas festivities, with all their family implications and associations, had left their mark on me. My back was giving me trouble and I was in such pain that I could hardly stand, sit, or move – perfect conditions for a therapy session! Eva asked me to draw this "problem situation". When I looked at the result, I could only nod in agreement. Yes, this was exactly how I felt: A tree bent from the force of the wind, scarcely able to stand erect, with roots sticking up in the air. Eva asked about when things were better for me and I drew another tree, standing straight with a solid trunk, crowned with shiny red apples.

Tree 1

Tree 2

I had more than a little difficulty managing the two basic physical components in NIG – standing and moving about the room. To my great surprise, however, standing on the sketch of the bent tree I felt well-grounded and solidly rooted. It was only in my upper body that I felt a slight swaying. The next surprise was provided by the apple tree. Standing on this sketch I felt light and warm in my upper body but at the same time I felt strangely rootless and lacking a connection to the earth.

I was confused and didn't know what to think, but Eva simply asked me to move to the meta-position and look at the whole thing from the outside. Standing in this position, I experienced the third surprise of the day. I suddenly saw the two trees completely differently! The bent tree now seemed filled with a deep knowledge of life. The straight standing apple tree, on the other hand, seemed hollow and proud.

Next, Eva pointed out to me that my eyes kept shifting back and forth between the two trees. I noticed a clear, tangible connection between the strong roots of the one and the beautiful apples of the other. In my mind's eye, the two different looking trees grew together into one. I saw the strength of the deep roots flowing up through the trunk of the bent tree to the fruit of the apple tree, feeding it and making it glow. I exhaled.

My eyes found the synthesis of these two seemingly irreconcilable polarities and then I began to understand. It was as if a curtain had been raised and it was clear to me how profoundly these two trees belonged together. I understood at a level that was new to me what it means to be connected to one's roots.

The year I had just come through was marked by intense work with constellations. I have much to thank my treasured teacher, Ilse Kutschera, for in this regard. During this time, I had seen and experienced again and again how much stronger the forces of fate are than my own strength of will, I had mobilized and utilized in my life up to this point. However, I had also experienced how much strength and stability I gained in accepting my connection to the power of fate within a larger context.

Now, as I stood in the meta-position in my first NIG session, looking at my "new" tree, everything the constellations had shown me was now present. I could feel the depth and the strength of my ancestors in the roots of the tree, which no longer looked bent to me, but rather leaning into life. I noticed how much the free-standing root helped give the tree balance. I saw how the fruit of my own personal life was fed from the strength of the roots and how hollow it seemed without that strength.

This first session with Eva Madelung was followed by a whole series of sessions which, despite varying degrees of intensity and topics, had one thing in common. The level of the archaic orders of relationship as they are manifested in constellations, and the biographical level of my own personal life ran parallel through them all and filled them with life. For example, in the next session, working with the "life path", it became clear to me which "next steps" I could take to move in the direction of my personal goals. Of course, I had already worked on reaching my goals in my years as a student and as a therapist in many other areas such as Applied Kinesiology, but what had been missing was, how different it was to know and experience this in harmony with my family.

"And did you leave the office free of back pain after this session?" some readers will be asking, having read the story of the two trees. No, the pain was not completely gone, but I walked out with a lighter step than I had walked in with. The next concrete step in my life was to find a body therapist, and since that time my back has been a trusty support, even at Christmas time.

Eva Madelung: A Short Personal History of Paradox

I think I was about fourteen when I first met up with the paradox of human existence. In German class we had read *King Lear* by Shakespeare and had to write an essay in class. Unfortunately, the content of my thoughts is no longer in my memory, but it probably had to do with the father's behaviour towards his three very different daughters. What I do remember quite clearly is that I had the feeling of having grasped something about the inevitability of human tragedy and I believed that I was on the track of a critical psychological factor. I was fascinated.

A few days later it was sobering to get my essay back with a barely passing mark written at the top. My German teacher, whom I greatly admired, looked questioningly at me as he laid my notebook on my desk. He asked me to talk to him later in the teachers' room. There, with a mystified look, he told me he couldn't follow my thinking. "It was as if you had thought too much and only written down every fourth sentence." Somewhat relieved, I explained as best I could what I had meant to say. He ended our chat with the friendly comment, "Well, now that you have explained it for me like that, it's easier to understand." The mark, however, remained as it was.

This exciting but sobering experience continued in the sometimes vehement arguments with my mother at that time. With the clear vision and arrogance of a teenager battling for autonomy, I saw clearly how much "egotism" there could be in a mother's sacrificial, caring behaviour. (That is what I called it at that time. Today I would more probably speak of blind primary love.) I could feel, on the one hand, how well-meaning she was in regard to me. On the other hand, however, I felt inordinately hemmed-in by her constant worry, which then drove me to act defiantly in some very worrisome ways. In addition, I accused her of not caring for anyone else in this way.

It took me a long time to notice how much I was hurting myself in my desperate need for autonomy, and I have learned a lot more through my own therapy experiences and those of others.

When I became acquainted with the systemic approach to therapy, I was delighted to recognize the major role of the paradoxical structure of the soul in systemic therapies. Beginning with Milton J. Erickson's brilliant and humorous way of dealing with the desperate need for autonomy, to Gregory Bateson's equally convincing observations on the "double-bind", to Mara Selvini Palazzoli's "paradox and counter-paradox", which was one of the factors that prompted me to write my first book about defiance (Madelung 1985).

For the pioneers in systemic therapy methods, it was clearly self-evident that with the best of intentions we move along the razor's edge between creativity and self-destruction; in an attempt to define ourselves, we inflict damage upon ourselves or upon others. It was also clear that there are constructive ways of dealing with this.

It was only later that it became clear to me that these paradoxes are also seen in family constellations as entanglements of primary love.

An excerpt from an unpublished lecture at a conference on hypnosis in 2000 in Munich:

"In general, hubris, the human tendency to overestimate one's own capacities and rebel, is seen as the core of human tragedy. Bert Hellinger saw this as well, and in the early years of family constellations he often confronted clients with their hubris in meddling in the affairs of their parents. Looking more closely, in the last ten years the focus of Hellinger's newer constellations has been the effects of bonds that underlie many tragic fates. 'The battle of love against the orders is the beginning and end of every tragedy.' (Hellinger 1996). In constellations, the basic orders are worked out – Hellinger calls it 'looking at how love flows' – and steps emerge that lead towards resolutions that were not previously visible."

Moving down to the level of archaic relationships and acknowledging these orders can relieve the double-bind situation of entanglements in family networks. What remains, however, is the paradoxical structure of human reality in which we are thrown back and forth between the drive towards independence *and* belonging, towards responsibility *and* surrender, between power *and* helplessness.

In many cases there is no option but to acknowledge and endure the irreconcilability of these contradictions. In doing so, a third solution may unexpectedly appear, or it remains open, as described in the following text.

It remains open

whether our view has meaning
for all this
remains open

whether the eye sees only itself
or the earth's sphere
with its crest of barren rock
spacious land
trees
greenblazing
the oceans
emerald
or the vastness of space
the sun
whirls of light spinning
spread far
the space
where time flows

remains open
if there is sense
in our senses

Looking Through Another's Eyes

To return once again to the pivotal metaphor of the systemic viewpoint:

As mentioned above (p. 46), Norbert Bischof has determined that children first learn between two and four years of age that other people see the world differently than they do. They learn, therefore, "to look through the eyes of another."

The Christian law to love thy neighbour and the Buddhist demand for empathy indicate how highly our spiritual values place this quality. It is also the basis for all dramatic creativity. Despite de Shazer's critique, (cf. p. 46), empathy is an essential therapeutic quality.

The invitation to try to look through someone else's eyes is, in my opinion, the essential message of systemic therapies. It becomes possible to go even further sometimes and imagine that it might someday be possible to look through the eyes of someone who is truly different, or to look with completely different eyes, and then to ask "who is actually doing the looking?"

Sometimes
it is
as if one could
between the eyes
in between through
outwards

and there is
to be seen what
is not to be
seen actually
as one
is it

not

oneself

(Both poems are from the book *ZeitLicht;* Madelung 2002).

Time and Eternity: Epilogue Scene

Stage setting: Open landscape. A path in the foreground leads over a bridge and exits the stage in the background. Two figures walk back and forth, talking.

Time: What do you think, really, about people? Perhaps I am getting old. It's getting increasingly difficult for me to understand them!

Eternity: *(laughing)* You, old? Look at me! But don't ask me about people. You're responsible for those details. I take care of the whole.

Time: *(stopping)* But perhaps you can help me out anyway. I just can't understand it anymore. Do they love me, or do they hate me? First they complain that they have so little of me, then they kill me whenever they can. Others put in a lot of effort and concentration in order to get away from me and stay only in the present. Can you make any sense out of these people? *(continuing thoughtfully)* You've got it made! The way I see it, you're very highly valued. They think well of you.

Eternity: If you only knew! It's much worse for me. They are afraid of me! *(unaffected)* It doesn't matter to me, though. I see the totality and I don't worry much about these details. But as to your question, I cannot make any sense out of that, and the way you describe it, these people seem to behave very foolishly. They don't seem to appreciate what they've got in you. As far as I'm concerned, I can't do anything for them. Nothing happens in me. But you, you are enormously useful for them. You let them be born, help them to grow up and to die. You put their relationships in order and allow them to find their way. You put balm on their wounds and heal them when they are in need. Isn't that right?

Time: *(in despair)* Yes, it is. Actually, I don't know why I give it so much effort, and I don't get any thanks. They scorn me. They want everything immediately. Sometimes that works when the time is right, but often it simply isn't. As hard as I try, and as much as I push myself, things just can't be done any faster. Some things take time. Some things take an eternity. Some things don't happen at all.

They remain standing on the bridge, look at each other and then both look at the flowing water below.

Eternity: There's one thing I don't understand about you. Why are these people actually so important to you? There are more impressive things. Stars, for example. People should be totally irrelevant to you. You could just go your own way.

Time: *(resigned)* If you only knew! *(whispering)* I am dependent on them. Completely dependent. I am their creation! *(louder)* You've got it made. You are simply there. Just because.

Eternity: *(thoughtfully, as they continue on their way)* I don't know about that, sometimes I doubt it. But for me – for me it really is irrelevant, you know.

We see the two figures moving off into the background, still talking, on the path that disappears from the stage.

Literature

Apel, K.-O. (1986): Das Leibapriori der Erkenntnis. Eine erkenntnisanthropologische Betrachtung. In: Petzold (ed.): Leiblichkeit. Paderborn (Junfermann), p. 47–70.

Bateson, G. (1972): Steps to an ecology of mind. New York (Ballantine).

Bateson, G., M. C. Bateson (1987): Angels fear: towards an epistemology of the sacred. New York (Macmillan).

Baxa, G., Chr. Essen, S. Essen (1999): *Praxis der Systemaufstellung* 2: 26–27.

Bischof, N. (2000): Das Kraftfeld der Mythen – Signale aus der Zeit, in der wir die Welt erschaffen haben. München (Piper).

Bökmann, M. (1999): Mit den Augen eines Tigers. Eine Einführung in die Methode der Tiefenentspannung in Gruppen nach Milton H. Erickson. Heidelberg (Carl-Auer).

Büntig, W. (1995): Die alte Person. [Lecture, Audio-Tape.] Münsterschwarzach (Vier Türme).

Cage, J. (1991): Composer John Cage. Konzepte wider den Zwang. *Du. Zeitschrift für Kultur* 5: 68.

Chopich, E., M. Paul (1997): Aussöhnung mit dem inneren Kind. Freiburg (Hermann Bauer).

de Shazer, S. (1988): Clues. Investigating solutions in brief therapy. New York (Norton).

Dilts, R., T. Hallbom, S. Smith (1990): Beliefs. Pathways to health and well-being. Portland, OR (Metamorphous).

Dilts, R., R. Bandler, J. Grinder (1985): Neuro-Linguistic Programming. Cupertino, CA (Meta Publications).

Erickson. M. H. (1980): The collected papers of Milton H. Erickson. Ed. by Ernest L. Rossi. Vol. 1: The nature of hypnosis and suggestion. New York (Irvington).

Franke, U. (2003): In my mind's eye. Family constellations in individual therapy and counselling. Heidelberg (Carl-Auer).

Hellinger, B. (1996): Die Mitte fühlt sich leicht an. München (Kösel).

Hellinger, B., G. Weber, H. Beaumont (1998): Love's hidden symmetry. What makes love work in relationships. Phoenix, AZ (Zeig, Tucker & Theisen).

Hellinger, B. (2001): Die Quelle braucht nicht nach dem Weg zu fragen. Ein Nachlesebuch. Heidelberg (Carl-Auer).

Hellinger, B (2002a): Der Austausch. Heidelberg (Carl-Auer).

Hellinger, B. (2002b): On life and other paradoxes: Aphorisms and little stories. Phoenix, AZ (Zeig, Tucker & Theisen).

Hellinger, B. a. G. ten Hövel (1999): Acknowledging what is. Conversations with Bert Hellinger. Phoenix, AZ (Zeig, Tucker & Theisen).

Hellinger, B., G. Weber, H. Beaumont (2001): Love's own truths. Bonding and balancing in close relationships. Phoenix, AZ (Zeig, Tucker & Theisen).

Innecken, B. (2000): Kinesiologie – Kinder finden ihr Gleichgewicht. Wissenswertes, Spiele, Lieder und Geschichten. München (Don Bosco).

Klinghardt, D. (1996): Lehrbuch der Psychokinesiologie. Freiburg (Hermann Bauer).

Madelung, E. (1985) Trotz. Zwischen Kreativität und Selbstzerstörung, menschliches Verhalten im Widerspruch. München (Kösel).

Madelung, E. (1996): Kurztherapien. Neue Wege zur Lebensgestaltung. München (Kösel).

Madelung, E. (1998): Trotz und Treue – zweierlei Wirklichkeit in Familien. Heidelberg (Carl-Auer).

Madelung, E. (2001): Ökologie des Geistes und Ordnungen der Liebe. Zwei systemische Sichtweisen im Vergleich. In: G. Weber (Ed.): Derselbe Wind lässt viele Drachen steigen. Systemische Lösungen im Einklang. Heidelberg (Carl-Auer).

Madelung, E. (2002): ZeitLicht. [Available at: Buchhandlung Avicenna, Amalienstr. 19, 80788 München, Germany; Fax: ++49-89-28 98 62 73.]

Ruppert, F. (2002): Verwirrte Seelen. München (Kösel).

Schlippe A. von, J. Schweitzer (2002): Lehrbuch der systemischen Therapie und Beratung. Göttingen (Vandenhoeck & Ruprecht).

Schneider, J. (1998): Familienaufstellungen mit Einzelklienten mit Hilfe von Figuren. In: G. Weber (ed.): Praxis des Familien-Stellens. Beiträge zu systemischen Lösungen nach Bert Hellinger. Heidelberg (Carl-Auer), p. 182–193.

Schottenloher, T., H. Schnell (ed.) (1994): Wenn Worte fehlen, sprechen Bilder. Bildnerisches Gestalten und Therapie (Bd. 2). München (Kösel).

Somé, M. (1994): Of water and the spirit. Ritual, magic, and initiation in the life of an African shaman. New York (Putnam).

Sparrer, I. (2004): Wunder, Lösung und System. Heidelberg (Carl-Auer).

Spitzer, M. (2003): Lernen. Gehirnforschung und die Schule des Lebens. Heidelberg (Spektrum Akademischer Verlag).

Stresius, K., J. Castella, K. Grochowiak (2001): NLP und das Familien-Stellen. Zur Komplementarität zweier Therapieansätze. Paderborn (Junfermann).

Ulsamer, B. (2003): The art and practice of family constellations. Leading family constellations as developed by Bert Hellinger. Heidelberg (Carl-Auer).

Varga von Kibéd, M., I. Sparrer (2003): Ganz im Gegenteil. Heidelberg (Carl-Auer).

Weerth, R. (1992): NLP und Imagination. Grundannahmen, Methoden, Möglichkeiten und Grenzen. Paderborn (Junfermann).

About the Authors

 Eva Madelung, Ph. D. After completing her studies in German literature and philosophy, Eva Madelung trained in primary therapy, body therapy, hypnosis, NLP, De Shazer short-term therapy, and systemic psycho-therapy according to Bert Hellinger. Since 1975 she has been in private practice in Munich and leads workshops in Germany and abroad.
E-Mail: EMadelung@aol.com

 Barbara Innecken, formerly an elementary and middle school teacher and speech therapist, received her training in applied kinesiology, psycho-kinesiology according to Klinghardt, family constellation according to Bert Hellinger, NLP, and NIG. Since 1994 she has a private practice as a therapist for speech therapy and psychotherapy near Munich (Germany), in which she specializes in kinesiology and systemic therapy. She conducts seminars and workshops and is the author of a book about kinesiology for children.
E-Mail: B.Innecken@web.de

Bertold Ulsamer

The Art and Practice
of Family Constellations

Leading Family Constellations
as Developed by Bert Hellinger

198 Pages, Pb, 2003
ISBN 3-89670-398-6

Using the systemic family therapy developed by Bert Hellinger, tensions and conflicts within families can be revealed. Through the use of representatives, the person involved can observe the psychic dynamics of his or her own family, and identify the patterns which are destructive. In his book, Bertold Ulsamer explains the basis of family constellations, considers the task and the role of the therapist in the field of subjective experience and objective knowledge. He addresses the use of language and the issue of dealing with emotions. His book is aimed at therapists and others who are interested in the practical applications of the Hellinger therapy.

www.carl-auer.com

Ursula Franke

In My Mind's Eye

Family Constellations in
Individual Therapy and Counselling

155 Pages, Pb, 2003
ISBN 3-89670-410-9

"In My Mind's Eye" is the first book about family constellations in individual therapy and counselling. The procedures presented rest on a broad range of therapeutic knowledge and experience from various psychological methods and approaches.

In the first section, Ursula Franke describes the foundations of her therapeutic work. The second part addresses the inner processes, questions, and decisions leading to interventions, that guide the therapist through the whole process of a constellation. The main focus is on the techniques of constellations in individual therapy, and on constellations in the imagination, which the author has developed over years of experience and observation.

"The repertoire that Ursula Franke offers here is astounding, but always clear and easy to understand in the richness of examples. It is a beautiful and useful book that has been long awaited. Congratulations!" Bert Hellinger

 **Carl-Auer Verlag**

Ursula Franke

The River Never Looks Back

Historical and Practical Foundations of Bert Hellinger's Family Constellations

176 Pages, Pb, 2003
ISBN 3-89670-391-9

"The River Never Looks Back" is a book about the theory and practice of the method of systemic family constellation. Ursula Franke provides a well-grounded historical overview of the precursors to family constellations. In addition, she presents and defines the central terminology of these methods. The author presents a hypothetical model that attempts to explain the efficacy of constellations and deals with a number of questions that emerge when actually carrying them out. The empirical section of the book allows the reader to take a look at the procedure that is used in the process of a constellation, from the therapist's initial hypotheses to the resolution stage of the constellation. Franke explains, step-by-step, the application in individual therapy. In addition, the possibilities for and limitations of using constellations in individual therapy are discussed.

The study presented in "The River Never Looks Back" focuses on therapy with anxiety patients. The results of the study can be used in regular psychotherapeutic practices, and is thus helpful for all therapists who work with constellations.

 **www.carl-auer.com**

Bert Hellinger

Insights

Lectures and Stories

138 Pages, Pb, 2002
ISBN 3-89670-281-5

This is a first collection of Bert Hellinger's lectures and stories now translated into English. In this book he allows us to confront without fear the deep issues of guilt and conscience and brings to light the hidden orders through which love within and between people and groups succeeds.

These stories attempt to lead us to a peaceful centre – a place where we can be collected and calm, in touch with our deepest love and longing, in tune with the world, and from which our relationships can be fulfilled and our lives healed.

This is a book of wisdom: exciting, moving and profound.

Carl-Auer Verlag

Now available!
New Tools
for Constellation Work
www.constellationset.com

→ Abstract Constellation-Set
24 Figures
in handy case
2 different sizes
(10 and 8 cm)
2 different genders
€ 198,–
Order-No: 2079

This extremely valuable constellation set is made of solid materials, compact, and comes in handy case. All figures are intentionally abstract in form, and come in neutral colors, so as to allow the entire focus to be directed to the relational system. They are also particularly good for setting up abstract elements, for example, in systemic structural constellations.

→ Playmobil-Set
40 Figures
in practical bag
Men, Women,
Children in diverse sizes and colours
€ 44,–
Order-No: 2078

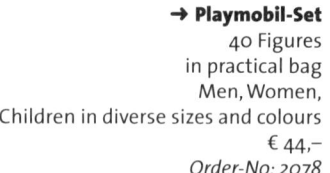

The 40 figures are immediately distinguished from the well-known play figures by their outer form, color and size. Five distinct colors allow the representation of different family, team or other system relations. Differences in clothing and hair color are also possible to allow for further differentiation. Differences in size allow the representation of adults and children, as well as hierarchical levels within an organization or company. The figure set is light, and therefore can also be used for external counselling appointments, workshops and training.